Vaping Home Brewers Recipe Collection
Volume 2

Vaping Home Brewers Recipe Collection Volume 2

Damien Smy

Kal Morris, Kevin Reed, and the members of Vaping Home Brewers

Vaping Home Brewers Publishing
2015

First Printing: 2015

ISBN-13: 978-1519331427

ISBN-10: 1519331428

www.vapinghomebrewers.com

Dedication

To my loving partner Jennie, and my children. Without your support, I would never have gotten through the harder parts of this project.

In remberance of my Father, 2 years gone, but not forgotten. Without helping you with your projects, I couldn't have completed these ones.

Contents

Acknowledgements

Acknowledgements for the VHB Recipe Collection series go to the members of the Vaping Home Brewers Facebook community, and Kal Morris, and the rest of the admin team for allowing the project to go ahead.

Further Acknowledgements to to Kevin Reed for his invaluable tips, tricks, and, yes, more recipes.

Foreword

I started vaping in the early days, before we now have all these fantastic juices that are out there. I never really got on with the pen type E-Cigarettes, and was very unsatisfied with the whole idea of vaping per se. After going back onto cigarettes and trying unsuccessfully to quite numerous times, I always sad I'd that if the asthma I suffered from childhood got worse I would quit for good no matter what.

Well, I went for an annual check up and was told I now was suffering from COPD (Chronic Obstructive Pulmonary Disease). Well that was the last straw for me and smoking after 35 years. I looked into the benefits of vaping and thought I would give it a go.

We are now 8-9 months down that journey, no cigarettes, and I have not felt better.

I now use a VW/VV device with a tank for day to day vaping and use a dripper for testing new juices I have mixed up.

I love the Vaping Home Brewers group, for the respect and help we get from the other members, and for me, most importantly the vast choice of recipes that we as a group have accumulated.

Many thanks to all those who have parted with their recipes and suggestions on this fantastic group.

Martin

Preface

Welcome to the Vaping Home Brewers Recipe Book Volume 2.

This publication has been a community effort, put together by members of the Facebook group Vaping Home Brewers.

Experienced home brewers are free to ignore most of the small tips that are there to help those new to mixing, as well as the warnings, as, after all, everybody will have a different style, and process towards their mixing.

If you feel you may be able to add to the group, it can be found by searching Facebook for Vaping Home Brewers, and requesting to join via the community page, as the group is now listed as Secret.

All Company Names are property, Copyright © or Trademark ™ of the relevant company, and are used without permission, affiliation, threat, or other derogatory use.

All these recipes are made through trial and error, and no guarantee is made that you will enjoy them as much as the creator.

Vaping is not recommended to those who have never smoked, and is intended to deliver nicotine in a safer manner than smoking.

All recipes that have been found in this publication can be found on the Vaping Home Brewers Facebook group, including either contributing member or source on where it was found. Unless otherwise stated, all recipes were created or found by Kal Morris, Admin of Vaping Home Brewers Group.

Cover Artwork courtesy of Paul Dolby

Dessert Style Recipes

WHITE SWIRL (NEW)
TFA Koolada 1%
TFA Vanilla Swirl 4.5%
TFA Vanilla Bean Ice Cream 5%
CAP Vanilla Custard v2 5%
Sweeten To Taste
....

APPLE FRITTER (NEW)
TFA Whipped Cream 2%
TFA Bavarian Cream 2%
CAP Double Apple 5.25%
TFA Cinnamon Danish 9%
Citric Acid Or Lemon Juice 1-2 Drops Per 10Ml (Optional) Sweeten If
Needed
....

KALSTER VAPES CUSTARD DE MENTHE (NEW)
CAP Vanilla Custard v1 8.5%
TFA Sweet Cream 2%
CAP NY Cheesecake 2%
TFA Creme de Menthe 3%
Sweeten To Taste
....

KEY LIME CHEESECAKE (NEW) Added By Danny Parry
TFA Key lime 10%
KH Digestive biscuit 6 %
CAP New York cheesecake 5%
TFA Graham cracker 3%
TFA Marshmallow 2%
....

ADDY'S YOGURT (Adapted slightly)
TPA Bavarian Cream 1.3%
TPA Blueberry Extra 3.3%
TPA Greek Yogurt 8%
FW Kiwi 4%
CAP Sweet Strawberry 5%
....

KALSTER VAPES STRAWBERRY CUSTARD (NEW)
FA Pear 0.2%
TPA Orange Cream 0.2%
TPA Dragonfruit 0.5%
CAP Sweet Strawberry 5%
TPA Vanilla Swirl 2%
CAP Vanilla Custard 7%
Sweeten To Taste

· ·

LIAR CAKE (NEW)
FW Caramel Candy 4%
CAP NY Cheesecake 6%
CAP Vanilla Custard v1 4%
Sweeten To Taste

· ·

KALSTER VAPES BLUEBERRY MUFFIN SUPREME (NEW)
FLV Blueberry Muffin 4.75%
CK Blueberry 1%
CAP Vanilla Custard V1 1.25%
TPA Bavarian Cream 0.75%
2 Drops Of Lemon Juice Or Citric Acid Per 10Ml

· ·

PINEAPPLE UPSIDE DOWN CAKE (NEW)
FW Yellow Cake 4.75%
TFA Pineapple 2.5%
TFA French Vanilla 1.75%
TFA Brown Sugar Extra 1.75%

· ·

BANANA CINNAMON CRUMBLE (NEW)
FA Banana 3%
TFA Bavarian Cream 4%
TFA Vanilla Swirl 1%
INW Biscuit 1%
FA Caramel 0.5%
TFA Brown Sugar Extra 0.5%
CAP Cinnamon Danish Swirl 3%

· ·

KAL'S STRAWBERRY WHIP (NEW)
FLV Vanilla Custard 6.25%
CAP Sweet Strawberry 6.5%
FA Meringue 2%

....

KEY LIME PIE (NEW)
TFA Key Lime 10%
TFA Graham Cracker Clear 4%
TFA Ethyl Maltol 1%
Lime /Lemon Juice 1 Drop Per 5Ml

....

MURRSTARD (MINT CUSTARD) (NEW) by Steve Hobday
CAP Vanilla Custard v1 8%
KH Murray Mint 10%
CAP Bavarian cream 3%

....

GINGERBREAD BRULEE (NEW) Chris Craig
CAP Gingerbread 8%
CAP Vanilla Custard V1 6%
CAP Caramel 4%
CAP French Vanilla 2%

....

KAL'S STICKY BLUEBERRY MUFFIN (NEW)
FLV Blueberry Muffin 4.25%
FLV Custard 2%
TPA Marshmallow 1%
TPA Sweet Cream 0.75%

....

KAL'S BANANA SPLIT (NEW)
TFA Banana Cream 6.5%
CAP Ripe Strawberry 6%
TFA Vanilla Bean Ice Cream 2.25%
TFA Bavarian Cream 1.25%
FA Marshmallow 1%

....

THE SOLVANG (Apple Waffle with Whipped Cream) (NEW)
TFA Belgian Waffle 7%
CAP Waffle 3%
FW Whipped Cream 3%
LO Apple Sugar 2%
TFA Bavarian Cream 2%
TFA Sweet Cream 1.5%
Ethyl Maltol 3 Drops per 10ml
Sucralose 1 Drop per 10ml
Steep 4 Weeks
....

SEQUONIA THRONE (NEW)
CAP Banana 7.5%
CAP Vanilla Custard 5%
TFA Strawberry Ripe 2%
TFA Coconut Extra 1%
OOO Pice Crust 1.5%
Sweeten To Taste
....

VANILLA CUSTARD CRUMBLE (NEW) Chris Craig
FLV Vanilla Custard 5%
TFA Cinnamon Sugar Cookie 4%
TFA Dulche De Leche 1%
TFA Vanilla Swirl 2%
TFA Graham Cracker Clear 1%
....

KAL'S GIMME A GOBLIN CUSTARD (NEW)
CAP Vanilla Custard V1 7.5%
TFA Vanilla Swirl 3%
FA Bilberry 3.25%
FA Nut Mix 0.5%
2 Drops Of Citric Acid Or Jif Lemon Per 10Ml
....

CLAIRE'S STRAWBERRY CUPCAKE (NEW)
CAP Sweet Strawberry 7%
FW Yellow Cake 5%
CAP Vanilla Cupcake 3%
TFA Sweetener 1%
....

CARAMEL CREAM (NEW)
TFA Carmel Candy 2.5%
TFA Vanilla Swirl 2.0%
TFA Graham Cracker Clear 6.0%
TFA Marshmallow 2.0%
TFA Vanilla Cupcake 3.5%

....

MINT CHIP ICE CREAM (NEW)
LO Mint Chocolate Chip 8%
TFA Double Chocolate 3%
TFA Bavarian Cream 1%
TFA Vanilla Swirl 2.5%
TFA Cotton Candy 0.5%
FW Sweet Cream 3%

....

DIVINITY WITHIN (NEW)
FA Tiramisu 8%
TFA Bavarian Cream 4%
TFA Whipped Cream 1%
TFA Sweet Cream 1%
TFS Chocolate 2.5%
FA Vanilla Classic 1.5%

....

DELICIOUS VANILLA (NEW)
CAP Vanilla Custard V1 or V2 1%
TPA Vanilla Swirl 1.75%
TPA French Vanilla Deluxe 1%
FA Vanilla Cream 1.25%
TPA Vanilla Bean Ice Cream 0.75%
TPA Vanilla Custard 0.5%
TPA Bavarian Cream 1.5%
FA Catalan Cream 1.25%

....

BANANA CUSTARD
CAP Vanilla Custard v1 5%
TFA Bavarian Cream 3%
TFA Banana Cream 7 %
TFA Whipped Cream 4%
EM 1%

....

KAL'S LEMON PIE (NEW)
FW Bavarian Cream 3%
FA Lemon Sicily 3%
TFA Pie Crust 3%
TFA Vanilla Swirl 2%
CAP Graham Cracker 2%
FA Whipped Cream 1%
1% EM

....

BAKER'S DOZEN (NEW)
CAP Vanilla Cupcake 10%
CAP Sweet Strawberry 4%
TFA Blueberry Extra 4%
TFA Toasted Marshmallow 2%

....

KAL'S PERT PEACHES (NEW)
TFA Peach 8%
TFA Vanilla Custard (or Swirl) 3.5%
TFA Cinnamon Danish 3.25%
TFA Sweet (or Whipped) Cream 2%
TFA Marshmallow 1.5%

....

STEVE'S MILK v4 (NEW)
TPA Bavarian Cream 3%
TPA Cheesecake (Graham Crust) 3%
TPA Key Lime 6%
TPA Strawberry 6%
TPA Vanilla Custard 3%

....

KREED'S MR KIPLING'S BRAMLEY APPLE PIE (NEW) Posted By
Kevin Reed
CAP Apple Pie 5%
TPA Green Apple 2%
TPA Sweet Cream 2%
TPA Pie Crust 1.5%
CAP Caramel 1.5%
CAP Vanilla Custard v1 1%
CAP French Vanilla 1%
TPA Dulce de Leche 1%
TPA Cinnamon Spice 1%
TPA Acetyl Pyrazine 1%
....

KREED'S KUSTARD (NEW) Posted By Kevin Reed
CAP Vanilla Custard 6%
CAP French Vanilla 4.5%
CAP New York Cheesecake 4.5%
CAP Ethyl Maltol 1%
....

PINEAPPLE UPSIDE DOWN CAKE (NEW) By Kevin Reed
TPA Pineapple 10%
CAP Cake Batter 5%
CAP Maple Syrup 2%
TPA Brown Sugar Extra 2%
Ethyl Maltol 1%
....

INSOMNIA (NEW)
CAP Chocolate Doughnut 5%
FW Butterscotch 7%
FA Coffee Espresso 1%
FA Meringue 4%
FW Yellow Cake 3%
....

KAL'S ORANGE CUPCAKE (NEW)
CAP Vanilla Cupcake 7.25%
CAP Sweet Tangerine 4.25%
FW Yellow Cake 4%
TFA Marshmallow 1%
I Find This Mix Works Best If You Don't Go Higher Than 65 With The VG Ratio

....

KREED'S THICK BANANA MILKSHAKE (NEW) Posted By Kevin Reed
TPA or DX Banana Cream 12%
CAP Vanilla Custard v1 5%
TPA Vanilla Custard 5%
TPA Malted Milk 3%
Ethyl Maltol 1%
The 2 custards do make a difference with the (DX) version of the banana. But if you don't have the TPA one then just use the Capella (v1) at 8%.

....

KAL'S APPLE PIE DELUXE (NEW)
FA Apple 1.5%
FA Apple Pie 1.5%
TFA Brown Sugar 0.50%
FA Butterscotch 0.75%
FA Caramel 1.0%
FA Catalan Cream 1.0%
FA Cinnamon Ceylon 0.50%
FA Cookie 0.50%
FA Custard 0.50%
FA Fresh Cream 0.50%
FA Pear 0.25%
FA Vanilla Tahiti 0.50%
FA Walnut 0.50%

....

KAL'S PEACH AND MANGO CUSTARD (NEW)
CAP Juicy Peach 7.25%
TFA Mango 7%
CAP Vanilla Custard v1 6.50%
CAP Coconut 1%

....

KAL'S WHIP YA NANA OUT! (NEW)
TPA Banana Cream 8.5%
TPA Bavarian Cream 2.5%
FA Coconut 2%
FA Cream Whipped1%
CAP Graham Cracker 3%
CAP Marshmallow 1.5%
....

GRANDMA'S APPLE PIE By Dom Murphy (NEW)
CAP vanilla custard v1 10%
FA Fuji Apple 6%
FW Cinnamon Roll 8%
CAP Bavarian Cream 2.5%
TPA Whipped Cream 1.5%
....

APPLE PIE & CORNISH ICE CREAM (NEW) By Tammy Duncan
CAP Apple Pie 10%
FA Fuji Apple 1.5%
INW Biscuit 1%
CAP Cinnamon Danish Swirl 0.5%
TPA Acetyl Pyrazine 0.5%
TPA Vanilla Bean Ice Cream 6%
CAP Vanilla Custard v1 1.5%
....

STICKY TOFFEE BANOFFEE (NEW) by Tammy Duncan
CAP Banana 6%
TPA English Toffee 7%
TPA Graham Cracker Clear 2%
CAP NY Cheesecake 2%
CAP Vanilla Custard v1 2%
FA Fresh Cream 2%
TPA Sweetener 2%
Just made this up with concentrates I have and adapted from 2 or 3 other
Banoffee recipes.
....

PINEAPPLE DREAM CHEESECAKE (NEW) By Tammy Duncan
CAP Golden Pineapple 5%
CAP NY Cheesecake 4%
FA Fresh Cream 2%
TPA Vanilla Bean Ice Cream 2%
TPA Sweetener 2%
Again this is adapted from other recipes.Feel free to use/change/share
....

KAL'S STRAWBERRY CUSTI (NEW)
FLV Vanilla Custard 3.40%
TFA Strawberry Ripe 2%
FLV Strawberry 2.2%
FLV Coconut 0.6%
TFA Bavarian Cream 1%
....

STICKY BANANA PUDDING (NEW)
FLV Vanilla Custard 3.00%
FA Banana 3.00%
TFA Banana Cream 3.00%
TFA Cheesecake Graham Crust 1.50%
FA Marshmallow 1.00%
FA Pear 1.50%
FA Butterscotch 0.75%
FLV Coconut 0.50%
INW Biscuit 0.75%
FA Meringue 0.75%
FA Vanilla Tahiti 0.75%
TFA Vanilla Swirl 1.00%
....

KAL'S BUTTERSCOTCH CUSTARD (NEW)
FLV vanilla custard 1.75%
CAP Vanilla Custard 7%
CAP French Vanilla 3%
TFA Butterscotch 5.5%
EM 10% Solution 1%
....

CUSTARD BISCUIT (NEW) By Steve Hollick
CAP Vanilla Custard v1 12%
INA Biscuit 2%
TPA Bavarian Cream 2%
TPA Sweet Cream 3%

....

CLAIRE'S COCONUT CREAM PIE (NEW)
INA Coconut 5.00%
CHC Devon Cream 2.00%
CAP Sweet Cream 3.00%
TFA Vanilla Swirl 2.00%
TFA Bavarian Cream 2.00%
FA Meringue 1.00%
FW Cinnamon Churro 4.00%

....

GRANDMAS PEACH COBBLER (NEW)
TPA Bavarian Cream 3%
TPA Toasted Marshmallow 1%
TPA Peach 5%
CAP Sugar Cookie 3.25%
TPA Vanilla Swirl 1%
TPA French Vanilla 2.65%

....

JAM ROLY POLY & CUSTARD Posted By Jay Fox
CAP Vanilla Custard v1 10%
CV Chef's Choice Jam Roly Poly 8%
TPA Raspberry Sweet 2%
TPA DX Bavarian Cream 2%
TPA Toasted Marshmallow 2%
FA MTS Vape Wizard 0.3%
Credit to Jcoo - http://juicemixingclub.com/recipe/jam-roly-poly-custard

....

HIC'S SUGARY ALMOND-APPLE TART
FA Apple Pie 4%
FA Marzipan 2%

....

KAL'S BLUE MUFFIN (NEW)
TFA Wild Blueberry 7.5%
CAP New York Cheesecake 2.5%
TFA Berry Crunch 2.5%
CAP Vanilla Custard v1 2.25%
CAP Brown Sugar 0.5%
AP (as a 5% solution) 0.3%
2 Drops Per 10Ml Of EM Or Ethyl Vanalin

....

BANANA CINNAMON CRUMBLE (NEW)
FA Banana 3%
TFA Bavarian Cream 4%
TFA Vanilla Swirl 1%
INW Biscuit 1%
FA Caramel 0.5%
TFA Brown Sugar Extra 0.5%
CAP Cinnamon Danish Swirl 2-3%

....

BRUTUS THE BARBER LEMON POUNDCAKE (NEW)
TPA Bavarian Cream 2%
FW Cake (Yellow) 5.5%
CAP Cake Batter 0.5%
CAP Vanilla Custard v2 1%
FA Lemon Sicily 1%
CAP Vanila Cupcake 2%

....

KAL'S RED CUSTARD (NEW)
INA Biscuit 1%
INA Cherry 1.25%
ANY Bavarian Cream 1.25%
DV Rhubarb & Custard 5%
CAP Sweet Strawberry 4%
CAP Vanilla Custard v1 3%

....

ASH'S BLUEBERRY MUFFIN & CUSTARD Created By Ash Ley
CAP Vanilla Custard 10%
TFA Cheesecake Graham Crust 1.5%
TFA Bavarian Cream 2%
FLV Blueberry Muffin 4%
FLV Boysenberry 1%

....

PEACHES AND ICE CREAM (NEW)
TPA Orange Cream 2%
CAP Peaches and Cream 7%
CAP Pear 3%
FW Ripe Strawberry 1%
TPA Vanilla Bean Ice Cream 3%
TPA Dragon Fruit 3%

....

BLUE CUSTARD
TPA Vanilla Custard 6%
TPA Blueberry Wild 6%
TPA Vanilla Swirl 4%
TPA Bavarian Cream 3%
TPA Sweetener 1%
4 Weeks Steep

....

Dessert Style

Flavour	Steeping Time
Apple Fritter	4 Weeks
Custard De Menthe	4 Weeks
Addy's Yoghurt	4 Weeks
Strawberry Custard	4 Weeks
Liar Cake	4 Weeks
Blueberry Muffin Supreme	4 Weeks
Kal's Strawberry Whip	4 Weeks
Kal's Banana Split	4 Weeks
The Solvang	4 Weeks
Sequonia Throne	4 Weeks
Kal's Gimme a Goblin Custard	4 Weeks
Claire's Strawberry Cupcake	3 Weeks
Caramel Cream	3 Weeks
Mint Chip Ice Cream	3 Weeks

Dessert Style Continued

Flavour	Steeping Time
Divinity Within	3 Weeks
Delicious Vanilla	3 Weeks
Banana Custard	4 Weeks
Kal's Lemon Pie	3 Weeks
Bakers Dozen	1 Week
Kal's Pert Peaches	4 Weeks
Steve's Milk v4	4 Weeks
Kreed's Mr Kipling Bramley Apple Pie and Custard	2 Weeks
Kreed's Kustard	3 Weeks
Insomnia	3 Weeks
Kal's Orange Cupcake	2 Weeks
Kreed's Thick Banana Milkshake	4 Weeks
Kal's Apple Pie Deluxe	3 Weeks
Kal's Peach and Mango Custard	3 Weeks

Dessert Style Continued (a)

Flavour	Steeping Time
Kal's Whip Your Nana Out!	4 Weeks
Grandma's Apple Pie	4 Weeks
Apple Pie and Cornish Ice Cream	2 Weeks
Kal's Strawberry Custi	2 Weeks
Sticky Banana Pudding	2 Weeks
Kal's Butterscotch Custard	4 Weeks
Claire's Coconut Cream Pie	4 Weeks
Grandma's Peach Cobbler	3 Weeks
Jam Roly Poly & Custard	1 Week
Kal's Blue Muffin	2 Weeks
Brutus The Barber Lemon Poundcake	3 Weeks
Kal's Red Custard	3 Weeks
Ash's Blueberry Muffin and Custard	6 Weeks
Blue Custard	4 Weeks

Fruit, or Fruit Style Recipes

CANDY SLAYER (NEW)
FW Blueberry Cotton Candy 8%
TFA Dragonfruit 3.75%
EM At One Drop Per 10ml
Citric Acid 10% Solution One Drop Per 10Ml (Optional Flavour Popper)
....

SUMMER LONGINGS (NEW)
FA Cream Fresh 2.5%
LO Strawberry 10%
LO Watermelon 5%
EM one drop per 10ml (optional)
Citric Acid or Lemon Juice One Drop Per 10Ml As A Flavour Popper (Optional)
....

WISHBONE (NEW)
Ectocooler 1.25%
TFA Pear 6.5%
TFA Strawberry (Ripe) 3.25%
TFA Honeydew Flavour 3.25%
Ethyl Maltol (Optional) 1 Or 2 Drops Per 10ml
Citric Acid Or Lemon Juice (Optional) 1 Or 2 Drops Per 10ml
....

KANZI INSPIRED (NEW)
TPA Black Cherry 1%
CAP Double Apple 6%
TPA Kiwi Double 3%
TPA Koolada 10% 1%
CAP Super Sweet 4%
FW Watermelon (Natural) 8%
....

KOOL FRUITS (NEW)
TFA Watermelon 7%
TFA Koolada 2%
TFA Strawberry (Ripe) 7%
TFA Pineapple 4%

....

KALSTER VAPES SOUTH SEAS VACATION (NEW)
TFA Lemon Sicily 2%
TFA Key Lime 5%
TFA Coconut Flavour 3%
TFA Banana Cream 10%
Citric Acid Or Lemon Juice As A Flavour Enhancer 1-2 Drops Per 10Ml
Only And Is Optional

....

KALSTER VAPES ICED STRAWBERRY (NEW)
CAP Sweet Strawberry 15%
Crushed Menthol 1-2 %
Steep 48 Hours For Best Results I Would Steep The Strawberry Alone Then
Add Menthol To Taste

....

APPLE DEW (NEW)
TFA Honeydew 3.25%
TFA Peach (Juicy) 3.75%
TFA Green Apple 14.5%
Citric Acid Or Lemon Juice As An Enhancer 1-2 Drops Per 10Ml (Optional)
Sweeten To Taste In Your Normal Way

....

SOMMER SOLSTICE
TFA Sour 1%
CAP lemon sicily 8%
TFA Organic strawberry 9%
Sweeten To Taste

....

MANGOBASE
CAP Sweet Mango 5%
INW Mango 5%
INW Cactus 5%
2 Drops Of Citric Acid Or Lemon Juice Per 10Ml Sweeten Only If You Feel It Needs It
....

JUICY CRUNCH BERRY (NEW)
TFA Berry Crunch 5%
TFA Strawberry 4%
TFA Dragon Fruit 2%
TFA Vanilla Bean Ice Cream 3%
Sweeten To Taste
....

SANDY BEACHES (NEW)
TFA Coconut 2%
TFA Strawberry 7%
TFA Pineapple 4%
TFA Watermelon 4%
Sweeten To Taste1-2 Drops Of Citric Acid Or Lemon Juice Per 10Ml As A Flavour Popper Is Optional
....

DRAGON DREAM (NEW)
TPA Banana Cream 5%
TPA Dragon Fruit 3%
CAP Sweet Strawberry 7%
....

KAMA'AINA (CHILD OF THE LAND) (NEW)
TPA Mango 4%
TPA Papaya 2.3%
TPA Pineapple 4.7%
TPA Sweet Cream 4.5%
....

TIGGER'S BLOOD (NEW)
TFA Watermelon 2.25%
TFA Coconut Extra 2.25%
TFA Strawberry (Ripe) 6.65%
Sweeten To Taste

....

EL CAPITAN (NEW)
TFA Coconut 2%
TFA Pineapple 4%
TFA Peach (Juicy) 5%
Sweeten To Taste

....

PINK BIRD (NEW)
TFA Strawberry 8%
TFA Peach (Juicy) 7%
TFA Coconut 2%
Sweeten To Taste If Needed

....

CACTUS MELON (NEW)
TFA Watermelon 8%
CAP Sweet Watermelon 2%
INW Cactus 2%
TFA Dragonfruit 2%

....

LIMEZINGA A Little Collaboration Between Barrie Hetherington And
Mixmaster Kal Morris
INW Lime 4%
TFA Pomegranate Deluxe 2.5%
Koolada 1.5%
2 Drops Per 10Ml Of Your Favourite Sweetener
1 Drop Per 10Ml Of EM
Warning:- It Has Been Noted That Some Citrus Juices Have Been Known
To Crack Acrylic Tanks So Glass/Pyrex Is Recommended

....

SLAPPED PEACH (NEW)
TFA Juicy Peach 6.5%
FA Meringue 2%
FA Marshmallow 1%

....

NANA CREAM (NEW)
LO Banana Cream 5%
TFA Dragonfruit 3%
TFA Strawberry 7%

....

POM POM (NEW) - A Cold Pomegranate Drink With Hints Of Blueberry
And Pineapple.
TFA Blueberry Wild 7%
TFA Pomegranate 4%
CAP Golden Pineapple 3%
Koolada 1%

....

PICKING BERRIES (NEW)
TFA Raspberry 3%
TFA Blackberry 1.5%
TFA Blueberry Wild 6%
TFA Koolada 1%
Menthol Liquid 10% Solution PG Flavour Concentrate 1%

....

KALAJACK (NEW) Kal Morris
FW Apple Jack 4.25%
TFA Berry Crunch 4.25%
FA Meringue 2%
FA Fresh Cream 2%
CAP Sweet Strawberry 1%

....

SWEET SUNRISE (NEW)
CAP Sweet Tangerine 7%
CAP Vanilla Custard 4%
EM 4 Drops/10ml
Lemon Juice/Sour 2 Drops/10ml
Vienna Cream 1 Drop/10ml

....

MANGO DRAGON (NEW)
TFA Mango 10%
TFA Sweet Cream 5%
TFA Dragon Fruit 5%
TFA Vanilla Swirl 3%
TFABavarian Cream 2%
Sweeten To Taste

....

KAL'S HONEY IN THE STRAW (NEW)
TFA Honeydew 4.75%
TFA Strawberry 4.75%
TFA Pear 1.25%

....

FUZZBERRY (NEW)
TFA Strawberry 5%
TFA Juicy Peach 5%
TFA Sour 1.5%

....

NECTA MAN (NEW)
TFA Nectarine 4%
TFA Mango 4%
TFA Strawberry 6%

....

STRAPPALOUPE (NEW)
TFA Strawberry 10%
TFA Cantaloupe 7 %
For an added flavour: Add TFA Pear 2% OR Mango (TFA) 2% and 2 Drops
Of Citric Acid Or Lemon Juice Per 10Ml Sweeten If Its Needed

....

PEACH MELON CREAM (NEW)
TFA Juicy Peach 9.5%
TFA Bavarian Cream 4.5%
TFA Cantaloupe 3.25%
TFA Vanilla Swirl 2%

....

FLAMINGO FREEZE (NEW)
TFA Strawberry 6%
TFA Juicy Peach 4%
TFA Mango 4%
EM 2%
Koolada 2%

....

KAL'S FRUIT IN A BASKET (NEW)
TPA Orange Cream 6.5%
TPA Mango 3.75%
TPA Strawberry 3.75%
TPA French Vanilla 3%
TPA Pineapple 1.5%
Sweeten If Required

....

STRAWBERRY BANANA YOGURT (NEW)
TFA Banana Cream 5%
TFA Strawberry Ripe 10%
TFA Vanilla Swirl 3%
Sucralose (Sweetener) 2%

....

POMEGRAPED (NEW)
TFA Pomegranate 7.5%
LO Grape 5%
Ethyl Maltol 2%
2 Drops Per 10Ml Of Citric Acid Or Jif Lemon

....

BLUEBERRY BOMB (NEW)
TFA Blueberry Wild 13.5%
TFA Vanilla Swirl 2%
TFA French Vanilla 2.5%
EM 1%

....

KAL'S THE GRAPE GATSBY (NEW)
TFA Grape Juice 9.5%
TFA Bavarian Cream 4.5%
TFA Pear 1.75%
TFA Apple Candy 2%
TFA Sour 1%

....

SWEET STUFF (NEW)
TFA Strawberry Ripe 4%
TFA Peach 7%
TFA Coconut 1%
TFA Blueberry 3%
TFA Cotton Candy 1%
2 Drops Of Citric Acid Or Jif Lemon Per 10Ml

....

FSANB (NEW) Alec
INW Blackcurrant 3%
CV Blackcurrant 4%
10% Citric Acid solution 1%
CAP Double Apple 4%
CAP Super Sweet 1%

....

SWK (NEW) Alec
TPA Black Cherry 2%
TPA Kiwi Double 5%
TPA Koolada 10% (Concentrate) 1%
FE Pineapple (Natural) 5%
CAP Sweet Strawberry 3%
FW Watermelon (Natural)1%

....

KAL'S BAVARIAN FRUITS (NEW)
TFA Bavarian Cream 9%
TFA Apple 3.25%
TFA Pear 2.25
TFA Banana Nut Bread 1%
TFA Marshmallow (To Taste, Use As A Sweetener)

....

GIRLFRIEND (NEW)
TFA Blueberry Wild 8.5%
TFA Pomegranate 8.5%
TFA Bavarian Cream 8% (Vanilla Swirl is an acceptable alternative)
Sweeten to taste.
....

KIWI CREAM (NEW)
TFA Kiwi Double 6%
TFA Bavarian Cream 5%
TFA Marshmallow 3%
TFA Whipped Cream 2%
TFA Sweet Cream 1%
....

KAL'S BANANA-AMAZIN (NEW)
TFA Juicy Peach 6.25%
TFA Banana Cream 4.5%
TFA Bavarian Cream 2.25%
TFA Marshmallow 1%
....

SNAKE BLOOD (NEW)
TFA Bavarian Cream 5.0%
TFA Coconut Extra 1.5%
TFA Ripe Strawberry 7.5%
TFA Strawberry 2.5%
....

THE MONKEY'S SNAKE OIL (NEW)
TFABanana (Ripe) 0.8%
TFA Bavarian Cream 8%
TFA Coconut Extra 1%
TFA Pear 4%
TFA Watermelon 1%
2 Drops Of Citric Acid Or Jif Lemon Per 10Ml
....

PINEAPPLE EXPRESS (NEW) Creator Dave Thorpe
TFA Bavarian Cream 5%
TFA Vanilla Bean Ice Cream 1%
TFA Coconut Extra 1.5%
TFA Pineapple 9%
....

MAN CREAM (NEW)
TFA Blackcurrant 9.0%
TFA Bavarian Cream 5.0%
TFA Vanilla Bean Ice Cream 2.0%
TFA Marshmallow 1.0%

....

KAL'S MUSKETEER JUICE (NEW)
CAP Sweet Lychee 7%
CAP Sweet Mango 4%
FA Mango 2.25%
FA Apricot 1%
TFA Green Apple 1.5%
FA Coconut 1%
TFA Orange Cream 1%
1 Drop Per 10ml Tart n Sour (LO) (Optional)
1 Drop Per 10ml Sweetener (Optional)

....

STRAWBERRIES AND CREME (NEW)
TFA Strawberries and Cream 10%
TFA Sweet Cream 2%
TFA Creme de Menthe 2%

....

FRUIT MEDLEY
LO Cantaloupe 3%
LO Strawberry Kiwi 4%
LO Blackberry 2%
TFA Whipped Cream 4%
TFA Banana Cream 2%

....

PLUTO (NEW)
TFA Honeydew 11%
TFA Pineapple 3% (Alternatively MBV, or FW)
TFA Papaya 2% (Alternatively MBV, or FW)
TFA Orange Or Ecto-Cooler 1% (Alternatively MBV, or FW)

....

JADE TIGER (NEW)
TFA Strawberry 7%
TFA Watermelon 5%
TFA Pineapple 4%
TFA Coconut 4%
2 Drops Of Citric Acid Or Jif Lemon Per 10Ml
12 Hours Breathing And A 7 Day Steep

....

PINEAPPLE SWIRL (NEW)
TFA Pineapple 3.75%
CAP Harvest Berry 3.25%
TFA Vanilla Swirl 2%
TFA Sweet Cream 2%
TFA Coconut Extra 1%
Sweeten If Required

....

MELONCHOLY (NEW)
TFA Honey Dew 6%
CAP Cucumber 5%
TFA Watermelon 3%
TFA Cantaloupe 1%
TFA Koolada 2%
TFA Sour 1%
CAP Juicy Lemon 1%

....

STRAWBERRY KISS (Keep It Simple) (NEW)
TFA Strawberry 6%
TFA Strawberry Ripe 6%
TFA Sweet Cream 2.25%
Sweeten To Taste

....

PUZZLE DUST (NEW)
TFA Pomegranate 3%
TFA Blueberry Wild 3%
TFA Cantaloupe 3%
CAP Sweet Watermelon 3%
TFA Cotton Candy 2%
TFA Sweetener 1% (TFA)
2 Drops Of Citric Acid Solution Or Jiff Lemon Per 10Ml

....

BERRYMELON BRAMBLE (NEW)
TFA Honeydew 3%
TFA Blueberry Extra 4%
TFA Pomegranate 2%
TFA Marshmallow 4%
2 Drops Per 10Ml Of Citric Acid Solution Or Jiff Lemon

....

BLACK DRAGON (NEW)
TFA Dragon Fruit 11%
TFA Blackberry 5.5%
TFA Sour 0.5%
TFA Pineapple 0.1%
Add 2 Drops Of Jiff Lemon Or Citric Acid Solution Per 10Ml
(Kal Note:) Not My Recipe Im Not Sure What Such A Low Percentage Of
Pineapple Actually Does Here Lol

....

WK CANDY (NEW) Alec
OOO Watermelon Candy 5%
TPA Kiwi Double 2%
FA Fuji Apple 2%
FA Marshmallow 1%

....

STRAWBERRY CREAM (NEW)
TFA Strawberry Ripe 6%
FA Vienna Cream 1.75%
TFA White Chocolate 2%
TFA Bavarian Cream 1%

....

STRAW COCO DRAGON (NEW)
FW Strawberry 7.5%
TFA Coconut 5%
TFA Dragonfruit 2.5%
EM 10% Solution 4 drops per 10ml

....

KAL'S STRAWBERRY SPLATTER (NEW)
TFA Ripe Strawberry 3%
CAP Sweet Strawberry 5%
TFA French Vanilla Creme 3%
FA Marshmallow 1.75%
Citric Acid As A 10% Solution 2 Drops Per 10Ml
....

BB'S JACKIN' PEACHES (NEW)
TFA Jackfruit 6%
TFA Juicy Peach 4%
TFA Blackberry 2.6%
TFA Sour 3% (Or 1 Drop Per Ml Citric Acid, Its Good Both Ways, Different
But Good)
....

LIME SKITTLES (NEW)
FA Lime Distilled 5%
FA Lemon Sicily 3%
FA Orange 3%
....

BLUEBERRY MALT (NEW)
HS Italian Cream 2.00%
CAP Vanilla Custard v1 2.00%
FA Fresh Cream 1.00%
TFA Vanilla Swirl 2.00%
TFA Cheesecake Graham Crust 1.00%
TFA Blueberry Wild 7.00%
FA Bilberry 1.00%
....

KAL'S SPACE DUST V2 (NEW)
TFA Coconut Candy 3%
CAP Sweet Guava 4%
TFA Key Lime 5%
TFA Watermelon 4%
2 Drops Per 10Ml Of Citric Acid As A 10% Solution (Jiff Lemon Will Also
Do)
....

MANGO RASPBERRY (NEW) By Ashley Carber
TFA Vanilla Swirl 4%
TFA Bavarian Cream 3%
TFA Philippine Mango 4%
TFA Sweet Raspberry 2%
CAP Vanilla Custard V1 6%
1 Drop Em Per 30Ml
TFA Marshmallow 2 Drops Per 30Ml
....

WATERMELON AND CHILL (NEW) By Danial Carcas
Candy Watermelon 13%
FW Koolada 2.5%
EM 0.5%
....

KAL'S MASSIVE MELONS (NEW)
TFA Watermelon 6%
LO Watermelon 3%
FA Melon Cantaloupe 2.5%
TFA Honeydew 3%
TFA Sweet Cream 1%
TFA Koolada 0.25-0.5%
....

PINK LYCHEE (NEW)
FLV Lychee 2%
FLV Pink Guava 3%
FLV Coconut 0.1%
FLV Cream 1%
....

BOYZ'N BLUE (NEW)
FLV Boysenberry 3%
FLV Blueberry 2%
FLV Cream 1%
TFA Plum 1.25 %
....

BLUEBERRY DANISH (NEW)
TFA Blueberry Extra 6.5%
CAP Sugar Cookie 5.5%
TFA Sweet Cream 3%
TFA Bavarian Cream 3%

....

COCO-MELON (NEW)
FA Coconut 1.5%
FA Lime Tahity Cold Pressed 0.5%
FA Lime Tahity Distilled 0.25%
FA Pineapple 0.5%
FA Watermelon 3%
2 Drops Per 10Ml Of Citric Acid Solution (Or Jiff Lemon)

....

ORINOCO (NEW)
TFA Pear 6%
TFA Pineapple 3.5%
TFA Jackfruit 2%

....

HONEYHONEY (NEW)
TFA Pear 6%
FLV Strawberry 3%
TFA Honeydew 2%
TFA Quince 1%
TFA Marshmallow 1%
EM 0.5%
(Kal's Edit:) This Isn't My Work But I Suspect That Amount Of FLV Straw-
berry Will Overpower The Other Flavours, If I Make It I Will Drop The
Strawberry Down To 2% Thats My Gut Feeling Anyway, I May Be Incor-
rect

....

KIWI HEAVEN (NEW)
FA Kiwi 4%
TFA Vanilla Swirl 5%
TFA French Vanilla 3%

....

STRAWBERRY PUFFS (NEW)
CAP Marshmallow 5.5%
CAP Sweet Strawberry 3%
FA Classic Vanilla 2%
TFA DX Bavarian Cream 0.5%

....

TWISTED STRAWBERRY
FA Sweet Strawberry 7%
FA Banana 7%
FA Vanilla Bean Ice Cream 4%

....

PINEAPPLE PUFF (NEW)
TFA Pineapple 6.25%
TFA Marshmallow 4%
TFA Bavarian Cream 3%
FA Coconut 1%

....

CITRUS ISLAND (NEW)
FA Mandarin 2%
FA Lime 1%
FA Lemon Sicily 2%
FA Coconut 1%
Sucralose 3 Drops Per 10Ml (Or Sweeten By Your Normal Methods)

....

MAMBO FRUIT (NEW) By Chris Craig
PS Black Mambo 9%
OOO Pineapple Peach 10%
Sweeten to taste

....

CAPELLA'S PEACH CUSTARD MK 1 (NEW) (With Assistance From
Rob Woodland)
CAP Vanilla Custard V2 8.0%
FLV Peach 6.0%
TFA Marshmallow 2.0%
TFA Bavarian Cream 2.0%
TFA Vanilla Bean Ice Cream 1.0%

....

FRUTITION - Created by Ash Ley
TFA Strawberry 5%
TFA Dragonfruit 3%
FA White Peach 2%
FA Fuji Apple 2%
TFA Vanillin 10% Solution 2%
INW Cactus 0.5%

....

DARK BERRIES (NEW)
TFA Acai 3%
FA Black Currant 1.5%
FW Cranberry 1.5%
TFA Champagne 1.6%
(Kal's Note:) Guess The Champagne Is To Give It A Little Fizz

....

DRAGON DREAM By Laura Marsland
TFA Banana Cream 5%
TFA Dragon Fruit 3%
TFA Strawberry Ripe 7%

....

ICY DRAGON'S DEN By Laura Marsland
TFA Dragon Fruit 8%
TFA Bavarian Cream 2%
Koolada 10% Solution 1%
CAP Sweet Strawberry 5%
TFA Whipped Cream 1%
EM 10% Solution 1%

....

WATERMELON AND STRAWBERRY MENTHOL By Helen H Green
CAP Sweet Strawberry 8%
TFA Watermelon 8%
Menthol 10% Solution 2-4%

....

Fruit Style

Flavour	Steeping Time
Apple Dew	48 Hours
Blueberry Bomb	10 Days
El Capitan	7 Days
Flamingo Freeze	7 Days
Iced Strawberry	48 Hours
Juicy Crunch Berry	7 Days
Kal's Fruit in a Basket	14 Days
Kool Fruits	48 Hours
Mango Dragon	10 Days
Pomegraped	7 Days
Strappaloupe	7 Days
Strawberry and Banana Yoghurt	14 Days
Summer Solstice	48 Hours
Sweet Stuff	7 Days

Fruit Style - Continued

Flavour	Steeping Time
Girlfriend	21 Days
Jade Tiger	7 Days
Kal's Banana-Amazin	14 Days
Kal's Bavarian Fruits	4 Weeks
Kal's Musketeer Juice	5 Days
Kiwi Cream	4 Weeks
Man Cream	14 Days
Meloncholy	10 Days
Pineapple Express	14 Days
Pineapple Swirl	21 Days
Pluto	21 Days
Snake Blood	14 Days
Strawberries and Creme	15 Days
The Monkey's Snake Oil	21 Days

Fruit Style - Continued (a)

Flavour	Steeping Time
Berrymelon Bramble	7 Days
WK Candy	24 Hours
Straw Coco Dragon	10 Days
BB's Jackin' Peaches	7 Days
Lime Skittles	7 Days
Blueberry Malt	4 Weeks
Kal's Space Dust v2	7 Days
Mango Raspberry	3 Weeks
Boyz'n Blue	10 Days
Coco-Melon	7 Days
Orinoco	7 Days
Kiwi Heaven	2 Weeks
Twisted Strawberry	2 Days
Pineapple Puff	3 Weeks

Fruit Style - Continued (b)

Flavour	Steeping Time
Citrus Isand	3 Days
Puzzle Dust	7 Days
Frutition	3 Days
Dark Berries	2 Days

Clone Recipes

JIMMY THE JUICE MAN STRAWBERRY ASTRONAUT (NEW)
TPA Apricot 3.5%
TPA Mango 1%
TPA Strawberry 10%
10 Hour Breathe
....

PINKMAN CLONE (NEW)
CAP Grapefruit 7%
TPA Key Lime 2%
TPA Lemon 3%
TPA Sour 1%
TPA Watermelon 5%
....

SEVEN SEAS CLONE
FA Blueberry 1%
FA Cucumber 0.6%
FA Strawberry 3%
FA Watermelon 5%
FA Spearmint 0.4%
....

MISS CHIEF (NEW) By Claire Collins
CAP Vanilla Custard V1 10%
TFA French Vanilla Deluxe 5%
CAP Toasted Almond 2%
CAP Hazelnut 2%
TFA Sweetener 1%
FA Fresh Cream 2%
....

CUTTWOODS MONSTER MELONS (CLONE) (NEW) Posted By Barrie Hetherington
TPA Cantaloupe 7.5%
TPA Papaya 7.5%
TPA Mango 7.5%
1 Drop Of EM Per 5Ml
1 Drop Of Preferred Sweetener Per 5Ml
....

ELEMENTS STRAWBERRY WHIP (NEW)
CAP Sweet Strawberry RF 14%
CVR Cannoli 2%
EM 1%

....

ROCKETMAN (But Better) CLONE (NEW)
EM 10% Solution 2%
TPA Blueberry Candy 9%
TPA Cheesecake (Graham Crust) 7%
TPA Dairy Milk 3%
TPA Greek Yogurt 4%

....

HYDRA - ZEUS JUICE CLONE (NEW)
DV Absinthe 7%
CAP Strawberry 3%
Menthol 10% Solution 2%
BJ Orange 3%
Mango 4%
VV Sherbet Lemon 1%
EM 2%

....

CUTTWOODS UNICORN MILK (NEW)
CAP Butter Cream 1.5%
CAP Graham Cracker 0.5%
CAP New York Cheesecake 0.5%
CAP Sweet Cream 1.5%
CAP Sweet Strawberry 8.5%
CAP Vanilla Bean Ice Cream 1.0%
CAP Vanilla Custard 3.0%

....

BABY PIGEON CLONE (ALPHA VAPES) Tweaked (Posted by Joe Nukem)
TFA Juicy Peach 8%
TFA Pineapple 5%
TFA EM 3%
TFA Dragonfruit 2%
TFA Menthol 2%

    The Original has Mango instead of dragonfruit but I didn't have any. But this is very nice anyway.

    They do one called The Dude - the same with the Mango without the menthol. Again, works with dragonfruit, but better with the menthol.

....

HOBBES BLOOD CLONE FROM THE VAPOUR CHEF (NEW)
TFA Strawberry 6%
FA Watermelon 3%
TFA Watermelon 3%
TFA Coconut Candy 0.9%
TFA Dragonfruit 0.75%
TFA Honeydew 0.3%
TFA Smooth 0.25%

....

KITE IN CLOUD. LENOLA CREAM CLONE (NEW)
LO Cheesecake 3.5%
10% Vanillin in PG 2.75%
INW Strawberry 1%
FA Coconut 2%
CAP Vanilla Custard V2 3%

....

KARMA CREAM FROM MR. GOOD VAPE CLONE
TFA Bavarian Cream 3%
TFA Cheesecake (Graham Crust) 6%
TFA Graham Cracker 2%
TFA Marshmallow 2%
TFA Strawberry Ripe 6%
CAP Peach & Cream 6%
TFA Sweet Cream 3%
TFA Graham Cracker 2%
TFA Acetyl Pyrazine 1%
EM 1%

....

SIMPLE VAPOUR CO. STRAWBERRY YOGURT CLONE (NEW)
TFA French Vanilla 1.5%
TPA Bavarian Cream 1.5%
TPA Marshmallow 1.5%
TPA Strawberry (Ripe) 5%
CAP Sweet Strawberry 5%
CAP Vanilla Custard 5%

....

THE PRINCE BY MONARCH (CLONE) (NEW)
TFA Fruit Circles 10%
CAP Lemon Meringue Pie 3%

....

JIZMOGLOBIN CLONE FROM GWAR / MBV (NEW)
TPA Blueberry Wild 4%
TPA Blueberry Extra 3%
TPA Sweet Cream 2%
TPA Vanilla Cupcake TPA 4%
CAP Hazelnut CAP 1.5%
TPA Sweetener 2 Drops per 10 ml
FA Vape Wizard 2 Drops per 10 ml

....

THUG JUICE FROM MOUNT BAKER VAPOUR CLONE (NEW)
FW Jungle Juice 13%
Shake, And You're Done

....

KOI FROM GEMINI VAPOURS CLONE (NEW)
TFA Honey Dew 5%
TFA Cantaloupe 4%
TFA Extra Coconut 4%
TFA Vanilla Bean Ice Cream 4%
CAP Butter 2%
TFA Toasted Almond 1%

....

KAL'S UNICORN MILK CLONE (NEW)
CAP Sweet Strawberry 8.25%
CAP Vanilla Custard 3%
FA Custard 2.75%
CAP NY Cheesecake 1.5%
FA Meringue 1.5%
FA Cream Fresh 1.25%
CAP Graham Cracker .5%
....

CARAMEL EGGNOG BY HEADINCLOUDS CLONE (NEW)
FA Vienna Cream 2.5%
FA Caramel 1.25%
....

TANJELLO FROM JAMESON'S CLONE (NEW)
CAP Tangerine 19%
TFA Marshmallow 8%
TFA Smooth 2 drops / 10ml
As with any citrus-based juice this one will cloud or crack plastic tanks.
....

EPICLOUDS MOM'S PINEAPPLE CAKE (NEW)
CAP Vanilla Custard V1 4%
CAP Cake Batter 3%
TFA Graham Cracker 3%
CAP NY Cheesecake 2%
TFA Pineapple 2%
....

TMAX SNAKE OIL CLONE (NEW)
CAP Juicy Orange 10%
CAP Anise 10%
CAP Juicy Lemon 8%
CAP Cool Mint 1%
EM 1%
....

THE VAPOR CHEF - BLACKPOM CLONE (NEW)
TFA Blackcurrant 10%
TFA Pomegranate 9%
TFA Lemon 2%
TFA Sweetener 2%
....

TWELVE MONKEYS KANZI CLONE (NEW) posted by Barrie Baz Hetherington
TPA Marshmallow 2%
FW Strawberry Kiwi 4%
CAP Sweet Strawberry 2%
CAP Sweet Watermelon 6%

....

GREMLINS VANILLA CUSTARD CLONE (NEW)
CAP Vanilla Custard v1 12%
TFA Vanilla Bean Ice Cream 5%
TFA Malted Milk 1%
TFA Bavarian Cream 3%
TFA Graham Cracker 3%
2 Drops Ethyl Maltol per 10ml

....

KAL'S OWN MUFFIN MAN CLONE (NEW)
FW Apple Jacks 8%
CAP Apple Pie 5.25%
FW Frosted donut 3.5%
CAP Vanilla Custard v2 2.5%
TFA Sweetener 2%
TFA Brown Sugar 1%
TFA Cheesecake Graham Crust 0.75%

....

XXX (BUCKSHOT) CLONE (NEW)
JF or CAP Kiwi 3%
TPA Juicy Peach 8%
CAP Sweet Mango 6%
EM 2%

....

TIGERSBLOOD SNOW CONE (NEW)
CAP Sweet Strawberry 5%
CAP Coconut 5%
12 Hour Breathe

....

SMURF JOOCE CLONE (NEW)
CAP Sweet Strawberry 9%
CAP Blueberry 10%
TFA Sweet Cream 5%
TFA Dolce De Lechee 2%
TFA Vanilla Swirl 3%
TFA Sweetener 1.2%
EM 10% Solution 1.2%

....

BRONUTS CLONE (NEW)
CAP Chocolate Glazed Doughnut 7%
FA Joy 0.75%
FW Yellow Cake 1%
INW Biscuit 0.75%
(Kal's Note:) Been Using This Its Very Nice I'm Tweaking A Little By Increasing The Yellow Cake To 1.5% And Adding 1.5% Of My Creambase

....

RIPE VAPES KEY LIME COOKIE
TPA Key Lime 3%
FA Cookie 1.5%
FA Lime Tahiti 1%
FA Catalan Cream 1%
Cap Sugar Cookie 0.5%

....

G2 VAPOUR PRIME DRUNK MONKEY
Cap Butter Rum 4%
TPA Ripe Banana 2%
TPA Vanilla 5%
TPA Sweet Creme 4%

....

D'OHNUTS CLONE
TPA Bavarian Cream 1%
TPA Cheesecake Graham Crust 3%
TPA Frosted Donut 4%
TPA Strawberry Ripe 3.5%
CAP Sweet Strawberry 3.5%
TPA Vanilla Swirl 3%
FA Vienna Cream 2%

....

ELEMENT FRESH SQUEEZE CLONE
FW Ecto cooler 15-18%
Sweetener* 1-3%
*The Sweetener Can Be Sucralose, Ethyl Maltol (Cotton Candy), Marsh-
mallow Or A Mix - Whatever Suits You
....

ALISA'S KRINGLE'S KURSE CLONE
TPA Creme de Menthe 3%
TPA Koolada 10% Solution 2%
CAP Menthol 2%
TPA Peppermint 8.5%
FW Sweetener 2%
Source: http://e-liquid-recipes.com/recipe/140696
....

BLACK ASTAIRE CLONE (NEW)
CK Loveable Liquorice 2.27%
CI Vimto Type 7.73%
VV Heisenberg 12%
(Kal's Note:) Apparently The Vimto Is Hard To Source But Its Available
From Vapegb And Mod-It Vaping Listed As Mellow High Concentrate
....

BLACK ASTAIRE CLONE By Karl Beavington
LL Black Currant 10%
FW Blackberry 10%
INA Eucalyptus 1%
CAP Menthol 3%
INA Aniseed 3%
TPA Sweetener 2%
Breathe 24Hrs 5Days Steep
This Is My Own Recipe But I Did Nick Ideas From Other People's Recipes
And Just Like To Say Thank You But Can't Remember Who They Are Or If
They In This Group
....

Clone Recipes

Flavour	Steeping Time
Strawberry Astronaught	10 Hours
Miss Chief	4 Weeks
Cuttwoods Unicorn Milk	4 Weeks
TMAX Snake Oil	2 Weeks
Blackpom	7 Days
Twelve Monkey's Kanzi	7 Days
Gremlin's Vanilla Custard	4 Weeks
Kal's Muffin Man	3 Weeks
Tiger's Blood Snow Cone	10 Days
Bronuts Clone	15 Days
Black Astaire Clone	5 Days

CHERRY MENTH
TPA Maraschino Cherry 8%
TPA Black Cherry 4%
TPA Vanilla Bean Ice Cream 2%
TPA Koolada 1.5%
FA Arctic Winter (Menthol Artic) 1.4%
....

BLUE DEW
TPA Mountain Dew 9%
TPA Blueberry Extra 8%
TPA Koolada 1.5%
TPA Sweetener 1.5%
....

OREO COOKIE
TPA Bavarian Cream 2%
LO Chocolate 5%
FA Cookie 3%
TPA Graham Cracker (Clear) 2%
TPA Peppermint (TPA) 1%
TPA Sweet Cream 1%
TPA Sweetener (Sucralose) 3%
CAP Vanilla Custard v1 3%
....

BARRATT'S REFRESHERS
TPA Rainbow Sherbert 8%
TPA Rainbow Drops 5%
TPA Sour 3.%
TPA Harvest Berry 1%
CAP Orange Cream 1%
TPA Strawberry 1%
CAP Raspberry 1%
CAP Key Lime 1%
Ethyl Maltol (10% SOLUTION) 1%
....

STARBURST
TFA Cotton Candy 1.5%
FW Salt Water Taffy 8%
TFA Sweetener 3.5%
LO Tart and Sour 1%
TFA Tutti-Frutti 6%

....

LEMON BARS
TFA Cheesecake Crust 3%
FA Lemon Sicily 2%
FA Vanilla Bourbon 2%
FA Custard 2%

....

NUT COOKIES
FA Nut Mix 1.5%
FA Vanilla Classic 2%
FA Caramel 1.5%
FA Cookie 2.5%
2 week steep

....

ON WITH THE SHOW
Koolada 1%
TFA Malted Milk 3%
TFA Vanilla Swirl 5%
TFA White Chocolate 2%
TFA Sweet Cream 1%
TFA Bavarian Cream 4%
TFA Creme de Menthe 1%

....

PEANUT BUTTER CUSTARD
CAP Vanilla Custard v1 12%
TFA Peanut Butter 8%
1 Drop TFA Sweetener Per 5Mls

....

STRAWBERRY CRACKER
TFA Graham Cracker 6%
INA Strawberry 4%

....

GRATTITUDE (NEW)
TFA Malted Milk 3%
TFA French Vanilla 3%
TFA Vanilla Bean Ice Cream 5%
TFA berry crunch 6%
1 Drop Of Em Per 10Ml
1 Drop Of Citric Acid Solution Per 10Ml (Optional Flavour Popper)
....

THINK PINK (NEW)
TFA Sour 2%
TFA Cotton Candy 2.5%
TFA Vanilla Swirl 3.5%
TFA Sweet Cream 4%
CAP Sweet Strawberry 6%
....

OOOOOOLALA (NEW)
CAP Sweet Strawberry 6.5%
TFA Banana Cream 2.5%
TFA Bubblegum (Juicy Style) 5%
EM 1 Drop Per 10Ml
Citric Acid Or Lemon Juice 1 Drop Per 10Ml (Optional As A Rounder And
Flavour Popper)
....

PUFF THE MAGIC DRAGON (NEW)
FW Blueberry Cotton Candy 7.25%
TFA Dragonfruit 3.75%
Citric Acid Or Lemon Juice 1-2 Drops Per 10Ml (Optional)
Sweeten To Taste
....

BAJA BLAST (NEW)
TFA Champagne 0.5%
TFA Key Lime 2%
TFA Blueberry Extra 5%
TFA Mt Dew Type 8%
Citric Acid Or Lemon Juice 1-2 Drops Only Per 10Ml (Optional)
Sweeten To Taste
....

BLACK AND BLUE ASTAIRE (NEW) - Chris Craig
TJ Black And Blue 6%
CJ Black Astaire 12%
For A More Menthol Hit Add 1-2% FJ Clear Storm.
....

KALSTER VAPES CRACKING TOFFEE (NEW)
FW Graham Cracker 6%
CAP Ny Cheesecake 4%
FW Butter Toffee 8%
TFA Bavarian Cream 1%
Sweeten To Taste
....

GINGER BEAR
TPA Brown Sugar 2%
FA Cinnamon Ceylon 0.5%
CAP Cinnamon Danish Swirl 4%
FW Cinnamon Roll 4%
FA Meringue 1.5%
NF Organic Ginger 0.5%
CAP Sugar Cookie 3%
CAP Vanilla Custard v1 3%
....

STAR (NEW)
FLV Lime 1%
TFA Strawberry Ripe 1%
FlV Coconut 8%
FLV Sweet Coconut 8%
TFA Vanilla Bean Ice Cream 4%

You can tinker with the ratio of the lime, as it is extremely strong. With the Coconut differences, the FLV Coconut is loaded with diketones, so that is something to be aware of, however, this is not true of the Sweet Coconut.
....

COCONUT BANANA CREAM (NEW) Chris Craig
TFA Coconut 6% (not double)
TFA Banana 4%
TFA Bavarian Cream 4%
TFA Dulche De Leche 1%
TFA Marshmallow 1%
....

HIESENBLOOD (NEW) By Steve Hobday
VV Hiesenburg 6%
KH Tigers Blood 15%
KH Lemon Sherbet 3%
....

MOON PIE (NEW)
TFA Banana Nut Bread 7%
TFA Chocolate 7%
TFA Toasted Marshmallow 3%
TFA Butterscotch 3%
....

NUTELLA (NEW)
TFA Bavarian creme 4.25%
TFA Bittersweet chocolate 3%
TFA White chocolate 3.25%
TFA Hazelnut 2%
TFA Peanut butter 2%
....

KAL'S CREAMBERRY IN STRAW (NEW)
TFA Ripe Strawberry 9%
TFA Sweet Cream 6%
TFA French Vanilla 3%
2 Drops Per 10Ml Of Citric Acid Or Lemon Juice
....

CLAIRE'S SPICED COOKIES AND CREAM (NEW)
CAP Cake Batter 2%
TFA Cinnamon Sugar Cookie 5%
FA Cookie 2%
CC Devon Cream 3%
TDM Spicy Bisquit 3%
CAP Sweet Cream 2%
FA Vienna Cream 1%
TFA Sweetener 1%

....

MUJA JUICE (NEW)
TFA Blueberry Candy 8%
TFA Pomegranate Deluxe 2%
DV Very Vanilla 5%
2 Drops Of Citric Acid (Or Jiff Lemon) Per 10Ml

....

MINT TIC TAC (NEW) Alec
FA Peppermint 2.5%
FA Anise 2%
FA Vanilla Classic 1%

....

KAL'S SPECIAL BREW (NEW)
TFA Bavarian Cream 9%
TFA Caramel 2.25%
TFA Peanut Butter 4.75%
EM 1%
TFA Marshmallow 1.5%
TFA Whipped Cream 0.5%
TFA Graham Cracker Clear 2.75%
TFA Vanilla Swirl 1.5%

....

KAL'S MILK (NEW)
TFA Vanilla Custard 7.25%
TFA French Vanilla 2%
TFA Bavarian Cream 2%
CAP Sweet Strawberry 1.75%
TFA Coconut Extra 0.5%
TFA Marshmallow 1%

....

BLUEBERRY SLURPEE (NEW)
TFA Blueberry Wild 6%
TFA Gummy Candy 6%
TFA Citrus Punch 4%
TFA Peach (Juicy) 2%
TFA Pomegranate 1%
TFA Sour 0.5%
1% EM

....

STARS ON ICE (NEW)
FW Kiwi 5%
FW Star Fruit 4.75%
FW Sour 1.25%
FW Extreme Ice 1%

....

RAINBOW NERDS (NEW)
CAP Sweet Strawberry 7%
CAP Raspberry 7%
CAP Super Sweet 1%
TFA Sour 0.5%

....

KAL'S A PEAR OF ACES (NEW)
LO Pear 7%
LO Watermelon 4%
TFA Wintergreen 1%
TFA Bavarian Cream 3%
TFA Whipped Cream 2%
EM 1%

....

KAL'S SICILIAN HONEY (NEW)
INA Vanilla 3.5%
FA Vanilla Tahity 3%
FA Lemon Sicily 2%
INA Honey 0.5 - 1%

....

KAL'S ORANGE CREAM (NEW)
TFA Orange Cream 10%
TFA Vanilla Swirl 5%
2 Drops Per 10Ml Of Citric Acid Solution Or Jiff Lemon
Em 2 Drops Per 10Ml
Based On A 65Vg/35Pg Ratio

....

WOBBLY CHOCOLATE (NEW)
TFA Double Chocolate (Clear) 8%
TFA Coconut Extra 1%
TFA Cotton Candy 1.5%
TFA Sweet Cream 5%
TPA Kentucky Bourbon 5%
TFA Caramel Candy 2%

....

KAL'S MILK V6 (NEW)
TPA Bavarian Cream (TPA) 2%
TPA Cheesecake (Graham Crust) (TPA) 3.25%
TPA Key Lime (TPA) 5.25%
TPA Strawberry (TPA) 6%
TPA Vanilla Custard (TPA) 3%

....

EL MONTE (NEW)
CAP Cucumber 6%
TFA Vanilla Swirl 5%
CAP Cinnamon Danish Swirl 2-3%
TFA Sweet Cream 2%
TFA Malted Milk 1%
Sweeten If Desired

....

LEMON DEW (NEW)
LO Lemonade 8%
FW Black Tea 7%
TFA Apple 1%
TFA Honeydew 1%
TFA Sour 1%

···

CHOCOLATE COVERED STRAWBERRY (NEW)
TFA Ripe Strawberry 2.5%
CAP Strawberry 8%
CAP Double Chocolate 2.5%
LO Marshmallow 4%
12 Hours Breathe And 14 Day Steep

···

ZOOCHBERRY CREAM (NEW)
10% Ethyl Maltol 1%
TPA Bavarian Cream 3%
TPA Coconut Extra 0.2%
TPA Dragonfruit 0.5%
TPA Marshmallow 1%
TPA Orange Cream 0.2%
FA Pear 0.2%
TPA Strawberry (Ripe) 3%
TPA Sweet Cream 1%
CAP Sweet Strawberry 6%
CAP Vanilla Custard 7%
TPA Vanilla Swirl 2%
TPA Whipped Cream 3%

···

KAL'S MASHA MIX (NEW)
TFA Watermelon 8%
CAP Sweet Strawberry 5.5%
FLV Raspberry 0.75%
TFA Blueberry Wild 2%
TFA Whipped Cream 1.75%
TFA Marshmallow 1%
FA Grapefruit 1%

···

KAL'S ECTO CREAM (NEW)
TFA Bavarian Cream 3.75%
Echo Cooler 4.25%
FA Vienna Cream 3%
FA Banana 2%
FA Marshmallow 2%
Sweet (Sucralose) 1.5%

....

KAL'S MONKEY TEARS (NEW)
FLV Peanut Butter 3%
FLV Banana 1%
FLV Blueberry Muffin 2.5%
24 Hour Breathing As Its Banana!

....

SPICED HOT CHOCOLATE.CHRISTMAS MIX (NEW)
TPA Dark Chocolate 1%
TPA Milk Chocolate 1%
TPAA Bittersweet Chocolate 2%
TPA Chai Tea 1%
TPA Cinnamon 1%
LO Marshmallow 4%
TPA Malted Milk 5%
TPA Sweet Cream 5%

....

KAL'S HONEY NUTS (NEW)
FLV Milk and Honey 2.25%
TFA French Vanilla 1.25%
TFA Peanut Butter 0.5%
FA Hazelnut 0.25%

....

DRAMA MEDICINE (NEW)
Anise 8%
10% Menthol Solution 3%
TPA Tutti-Frutti 2%

....

MILLIONAIRES ELIXIR (NEW) Posted By Robert Robert
FA Fruit Circles 5%
FA Irish Cream 3%
TPA Dairy Milk 4%
Dulce De Leche 5%
CAP Peaches And Cream 2.5%
CAP Sweet Tangerine 3%
CAP Cinnamon Danish Swirl 2%
CAP Graham Cracker Clear 1%
FW Vanilla Cupcake 2%
....

KAL'S MORONIC ADMIRERS (NEW)
TFA Ripe Strawberry 7%
CAP V1 Vanilla Custard 3.5%
LO Banana Cream 4%
TFA Cheesecake Graham Crust 3%
TFA Bavarian Cream 1.5%
....

KAL'S RATHER NICE NANA-ICE (NEW)
TPA Banana Cream 7%
FW Vanilla Bean Ice Cream 7%
TPA Coconut 2%
TPA Koolada 10% Solution 3%
....

HOLIDAY EGGNOG (NEW)
FW or Cap Eggnog 6%
FA Jamaican Rum 1.5%
FA Marzipan 1%
TFA Brown Sugar (Extra) 2.5%
FA Cinnamon Ceylon .3%
FA Catalan Cream 1.5%
....

SNOWDROP (NEW)
CAP Peppermint 9%
TFA Vanilla Swirl 5%
TFA Sweet Cream 5%
TFA Koolada 2%
TFA Ethyl Maltol 10% Solution 1%
TFA Marshmallow 1%
....

BOURBON BUTTERSCOTCH RIPPLE (NEW)
TFA Butterscotch 4%
FA Cinnamon Ceylon 0.5%
TFA Sweet Cream 2%
TFA Vanilla Bean Ice Cream 5%
FA Vanilla Bourbon 2%

....

GINGER CREAM COOKIE (NEW) By Tammy Duncan
CAP Gingerbread 7.5%
INW Biscuit 2%
TPA Bavarian Cream 2%
TPA Sweet Cream 2%
TPA Graham Cracker Clear 2%
CAP Vanilla Custard v1 3%
TPA White Chocolate 1%
TPA Pumpkin Spice 0.5%
(Tammy's Note:) Tastes good after 2 weeks but I'm going to leave it for 4
and see if it improves. Might up the gingerbread or change the pumpkin
spice for ginger.

....

YELLOW SNOW (NEW) By Tammy Duncan
CAP Cool Mint 7%
CAP Vanilla Custard v1 4%
TPA English Toffee 4%

....

PINK SHORTCAKE (NEW) By Tammy Duncan
TPA Strawberry Ripe 6%
CLA Rich Rhubarb 3%
INW Biscuit 2%
TPA Bavarian Cream 2%
Ethyl Maltol 2%

....

SHERBET FOUNTAIN (NEW) By Richard Harkness
TPA Rainbow Sherbet 11%
FW Black Liquorice 5%
CAP Sweet Cream 2%
TPA Sour 1%
TPA Sweetener 1%

....

BANSIDHE BLUE (NEW)
FLV Blueberry Muffin 3.5%
FLV Coconut 0.4%
FLV Coffee 1%
FLV Virginia Tobacco 1%

....

BUTTERSCOTCH APPLE (NEW)
TPA Apple 8%
TPA Butterscotch 7%
TPA Cheesecake (Graham Crust) 2.25%

....

SUICIDE KAL (NEW)
TFA Vanilla Custard 3.5%
CAP Vanilla Custard V1 4%
FLV Vanilla Custard 1.25%
CAP Cake Batter 4%
TPA Yellow Cake 2.5%
FW Vanilla Bean Ice Cream 1.25%
TFA Sweet Cream 2%
TFA Bavarian Cream 3%

....

FAIRE PLAY (NEW)
FW Caramel Candy 4%
FA Fuji 3%
TFA Caramel Original 2%
FW or TFA Hazelnut 2%
TFA Peanut Butter 1%
TFA Marshmallow 1%

....

KAL'S GREEN GODDESS
BJ The Grinch 8%
VV Heisenberg 7%
KH Aniseed 2%
Ethyl Maltol Add 2 Drops Per 10Ml Only

....

WHATSITWHOSIT (NEW)
TFA Strawberries and Cream 7%
TFA Berry Crunch 3%
TFA Marshmallow 3%
FE Raspberry 2%
TFA Bavarian Cream 2%
CAP Vanilla Custard V1 2%

....

BOOBY BISCUIT (NEW) By Danny Parry
TFA Strawberry Ripe 6%
CAP Vanilla Custard V1 6%
KH Digestive Biscuit 6%

....

CUSTARD CREAM BISCUIT (NEW) By Phil Garret
CAP Vanilla Custard V1 12%
FA Whipped Cream 3%
FW Graham Cracker 3%
FA Bavarian Cream 2%
CAP Butter 1%

....

KAL'S BACK ON TRACK (NEW)
CAP Vanilla Custard V1 4%
TFA Sweet Cream 2.75%
TFA Bavarian Cream 2%
TFA Watermelon 4%
TFA Pineapple 3%

....

STATE FAIR (NEW)
Acetyl Pyrazine 0.5%
FA Almond 1.5%
FA Caramel 3%
FA Cookie 1%
FA Fuji 4%

....

KAL'S STRAWBERRY SHORTCAKE (NEW)
TFA Strawberry Ripe 3.5%
TFA Strawberry 2%
TFA Bavarian Cream 2%
TFA Vanilla Swirl 2%
CAP Sugar Cookie 2%
INW Biscuit 2%
TFA Cheesecake Graham Crust 1.5%
FW Yellow Cake 1.25%
CAP Marshmallow 1%
(Kal's Note:) Sweeten Only If You Feel It Needs It And No Additives Required

....

MAD HATTER (NEW) By Steve Hobday
KH Mango 3%
FA Anise 5%
TFA Horehound 1%
FW Ecto Cooler 12%
KH Lemon Sherbet 2%
KH Eucalyptus 0.5%
Sweetener 4%

....

TOP OF NEW YORK (NEW)
CAP Waffle 7.00%
CAP Graham Cracker 0.50%
FA Meringue 0.75%
CAP Cinnamon Danish 0.50%
TFA Bananas Foster 1.00%
CAP New York Cheesecake 0.75%
FA Maple Syrup 0.25%

....

GURI-GURI V3 (NEW)
FA Cream Fresh 3%
FA Lemon Sicily 1.2%
FA Lime Tahity Cold Pressed 0.5%
TPA Marshmallow 0.75%
TPA Strawberry 2%
TPA Sweet Cream 0.75%
CAP Sweet Guava 2%
CAP Sweet Strawberry 1.5%
FA Vienna Cream 2%
FW Yogurt 2%

....

GAZELLE HORN (NEW)
FA Marzipan 2%
FA Almond 1%
FA Orange 0.5%
TFA Orange Cream 1%
FA Cinnamon Ceylon 1%
FA Meringue 1%

....

BLACK DAY (NEW)
INA Anise 2%
INA Liquorice 6%
INA Mentol 1%
INA Raspberry 3%
TPA Sweetener 1%
TPA Whipped Cream 2%

....

THE DUDE (NEW)
FA Fresh Cream 2%
FA Tiramisu 1%
FA Vienna Cream 1%
TFA Milk 1.5%
FA Jamaica Rum 1%
FA Chocolate 2.25%
FA Cocoa 0.25%

....

CHRISTMAS BISCUITS (NEW)
TPA Cinnamon Spice 2%
TPA DX Hazelnut 5%
TPA Milk Chocolate 5%
TPA Orange Mandarin 5%
....

RASPBERRY CHOCOLATES (NEW)
INW Chocolate Cream 2%
TFA Double Chocolate (Clear) 3%
INW Raspberry 1.4%
FA Forest Fruit 0.75%
FLV Milk and Honey 0.75%
....

GINGERBREAD COOKIE (NEW)
TFA Gingerbread Cookie 5%
FA Cookie 1.5%
INW Biscuit 1%
EM 0.5%
....

BLU MINT By Luke Davies
CAP Blueberry 4%
TPA Peppermint 5%
CAP Blue Raspberry Cotton Candy 4%
TPA Koolada 10% Solution 1%
INA Menthol 10 % Solution 1%
....

BLUE SLUSH PUPPY By Grantley Oliver
VD Blue Slush 10%
CVR Blue Raspberry 10%
MTS Vape Wizard 1 Drop Per 10ml
EM 10% Solution 1 Drop Per 10ml
....

Miscellaneous Recipes

Flavour	Steeping Time
Nut Cookies	2 Weeks
Puff the Magic Dragon	2 Weeks
Baja Blast	1 Week
Cracking Toffee	2 Weeks
Coconut Banana Cream	2 Weeks
Hiesenblood	1 Week
Kal's Creamberry in Straw	4 Weeks
Muja Juice	1 Week
Kal's Special Brew	4 Weeks
Kal's Milk	4 Weeks
Blueberry Slurpee	1 Week
Stars on Ice	5 Days
Rainbow Nerds	5 Days
Kal's A Pear of Aces	5 Days

Miscellaneous Recipes Continued

Flavour	Steeping Time
Kal's Sicilian Honey	2 Weeks
Kal's Orange Cream	3 Weeks
Wobbly Chocolate	4 Weeks
Kal's Milk V6	4 Weeks
Chocolate Covered Strawberry	2 Weeks
Zoochberry Cream	3 Weeks
Kal's Monkey Tears	2 Weeks
Kal's Honey Nuts	10 Days
Drama Medicine	1 Week
Millionaires Elixir	12 Days
Kal's Moronic Admirers	4 Weeks
Kal's Rather Nice Nana-Ice	1 Week
Bourbon Butterscotch Ripple	2 Weeks
Ginger Cream Cookie	4 Weeks

Miscellaneous Recipes Continued-1

Flavour	Steeping Time
Sherbert Fountain	1 Week
Bansidhe Blue	10 Days
Butterscotch Apple	2 Weeks
Suicide Kal	4 Weeks
Faire Play	2 Weeks
Whatsitwhosit	2 Weeks
Booby Biscuit	3 Weeks
Kal's Back On Track	3 Weeks
State Fair	Overnight
Kal's Strawberry Shortcake	5 Weeks
Top of New York	2 Weeks
Guri-Guri	4 Weeks
Raspberry Chocolates	10 Days

Drink or Alcohol Inspired Recipes

BOURBON SMOOTH
TPA Kentucky Bourbon 9%
TPA Vanilla Swirl 3%
TPA Toasted Marshmallow 1.5%

....

CREAMY PINA
TFA Pina Colada 5%
TFA Pineapple 6%
TFA Sweet Cream 2%
Sour 0.5%
EM 0.5%

....

EARL GREY WITH HONEY
TFA Earl Grey Tea 5%
TFA Honey 5%

....

JAMACIAN COLA
FA Coconut 1%
FA Cola 3%
FA Jamaican Rum 2%

....

TRIPLE MELON LEMONADE
CAP Cantaloupe 3.5%
CAP Honeydew Melon 3%
TFA Lemon 5.5%
CAP Sweet Watermelon 4%
TFA Sweetener 2.5%
LO Tart and Sour 1.5%

....

BLACKBERRY BRANDY
TFA Blackberry 7%
TFA/FW Brandy 5%
TFA/FWHoney 2%
TFA Lemon 1%
TFA Sweetener 3%

....

MOUNTAIN COLA
TFA Citrus Punch 8%
TFA Cola 4%
TFA Energy Drink 2%
TFA Sweetener 0.5%

....

PINEAPPLE TEA
TFA Pineapple (TFA) 8%
TFA Earl Grey (TFA) 2%
TFA Ethyl Maltol (TFA) 1%

....

BAILEYS
EM 10% Solution 1.5%
FA Fresh Cream 1.5%
FA Malted Milk 1%
FA Whiskey 1.5%
INW Chocolate Cream 5%

....

BLUE CHAMPAGNE (NEW)
TFA Whipped Cream 6%
TFA Blueberry Flavour (Extra) 10%
TFA Champagne 7.5%
Citric Acid Or Lemon Juice1-2 Drops Only Per 10Ml
(Optional) Sweeten To Taste

....

COCONUT STRAWBERRY VANILLA SHAKE (NEW) Chris Craig
TFA Strawberry Ripe 7%
OOO Coconut Milk 5%
OOO Vanilla Shake 5%
TFA Coconut 2%
TFA Marshmallow 1%
....

GREEN PEACH TEA (NEW)
TFA Juicy Peach 10%
TFA Green Tea 5%
TFA Coconut Candy 1% (Enhances Peach, optional)
....

RUM RUNNER (NEW)
TFA Banana Ripe 4%
TFA Blackberry 3%
TFA Pineapple 2%
FA Jamaican Rum 2%
LO Tart 'n' Sour 2%
FA Mandarin 1.5%
TFA Citrus Punch 1%
FA Brandy 1%
FA Pomegranate 0.5%
....

KAL'S RASPBERRY LEMONADE (NEW)
LO Lemonade 8.75%
LO Raspberry 7%
Citric Acid Or Jiff Lemon 2 Drops Per 10Ml
My Mixes Are Based On A 65/35 Vg/Pg Ratio So Percentages May Need To
Be Tweaked If Going Higher Vg
....

PERP'S COFFEE
CAP Cup of Joe 12%
TPA Caramel (Original) 8%
CCW Cream 0.5%
TPA Sweetener 1%
http://allaboute-cigarettes.proboards.com/thread/57898/capella-cup-joe-percentage-suggestion

....

RASPBERRY LEMONADE (PAULA'S MIX) (NEW)
FA Lemon Sicily 4%
CAP Juicy Lemon 1%
INW Raspberry 2.5%
FA Lime Cold Pressed 0.5%
FA Meringue 0.35%
TFA Champagne 1%
TFA Sour 0.5%
Ethyl Maltol 2 Drops Per 10Ml

....

FRUIT SMOOTHIE (NEW)
TFA Banana Cream 6%
TFA Strawberry 8%
FA Mandarin 2%
CAP Coconut 1%
3 Week Steep

....

KAL'S GRANDMA WE LOVE YOU (NEW)
CHV Grandmas lemonade 6%
TPA Orange Mandarin 5%
TFA Strawberry ripe 6%
2 Drops Of Citric Acid Solution Or Jiff Lemon Per 10Ml

....

VIMTO By Keith Jury
FA Blackcurrant 8%
INA Grape 4%
INA Raspberry 6%

....

Drink, or Alcohol Inspired Recipes

Flavour	Steeping Time
Earl Grey with Honey	2 Weeks
Triple Melon Lemonade	1 Week
Blue Champagne	2 Weeks
Coconut Strawberry Vanilla Shake	1 Week
Rum Runner	10 Days
Kal's Raspberry Lemonade	5 Days
Raspberry Lemonade (Paula's Mix)	1 Week
Kal's Grandma We Love You	1 Week

SMOKEY DONUT
CAP Chocolate Glazed Doughnut 5%
TFA Black Honey Tobacco 4%

....

TURKISH BLEND (NEW)
TFA Turkish 10%
TFA Double Chocolate Clear 3%
CAP Expresso 3%
LO Bavarian Cream 3%
TFA RY4 Double 2%
2 Weeks Steeping

....

DANISH TOBACCO (NEW)
TFA Cinnamon Danish 5%
TFA RY4 Double Flavour 10%

....

BANANA NUT TOBACCO (NEW)
TPA Banana Cream 11%
TPA Hazelnut 3.5%
TPA Toasted Almond 3%
FA 7 Leaves 1%
2 Drops per 10ml MTS Vape Wizard

....

RY FOREVER (NEW) Chris Craig
TFA RY4 Asian 6%
CAP Vanilla Custard V1 2%
TFA Dulche De Leche 2%
TFA Hazelnut Praline 2%
CAP Banana 2%

....

BLUEBERRY DUTCH (NEW)
SM English Tobacco 6%
TFA BlueBerry 3%
TFA Mary Jane 1%

....

GINGERBREAD BACKY Martin Hinchliffe
FA Golden Rollie 2%
Cap Gingerbread 5%
MTS Vape Wizard 1%

....

KREED'S BACCY (NEW) Posted By Kevin Reed
TPA DK Tobacco - 3%
TPA Kentucky Bourbon - 3%
TPA Hazelnut - 3%
CAP Caramel - 3%
CAP Marshmallow - 2%
TPA Acetyl Pyrazine - 1%
Saline (0.9%) 2 drops per 10ml

....

DOUBLEMISU (NEW)
TFA RY4 Double 3%
FA Virginia 0.5%
FA Tiramisu 1%
FA Catalan Cream 1%

....

HIC'S TOSCANELLO FONDENTE CIGAR (NEW)
2% FA Tuscan Reserve
2% FA Cocoa

....

Tobacco Recipes

Flavour	Steeping Time
Turkish Blend	2 Weeks
RY Forever	1 Week
Gingerbread Backy	10 Days
Kreeds Baccy	2 Weeks

GOLDEN GRAHAMS WITH MILK (NEW)
TFA Brown Sugar 0.50%
FA Catalan Cream 1%
TFA Cheesecake with Graham Crust 1%
FA Cinnamon Ceylon 1%
FA Cookie 1%
TFA Graham Cracker Clear 2%
FW Hazelnut 1.5%
FA Honey (10% Solution) 1.25%
FA Marzipan 0.5%
FA Meringue 1.5%
FW Yellow Cake 1.5%

STRAWBERRY YOGHURT CHEESECAKE (NEW)
INW Biscuit 0.75%
TPA Cheesecake (Graham Crust) 1 %
CAP Graham Cracker 0.5 %
TPA Strawberry 1.75 %
CAP Sweet Strawberry 4.25%
FW Yogurt 3.25 %
Sweeten To Taste

MUSTARD MILK Simple Strawberries and Cream
TPA Strawberry 6%
TPA Vanilla Bean Ice Cream 8%
http://e-liquid-recipes.com/recipe/104221

MUSTARD MILK V2 - Simple diketone-free Strawberries and Cream
FA Fresh Cream 1%
TPA French Vanilla 2%
TPA Strawberry 6%
TPA Vanilla Bean Gelato 4%
http://e-liquid-recipes.com/recipe/143350

EXOTIC PEACH YOGURT
FLV Peach 3%
FLV Pink Guava 2%
FLV Greek Yogurt 2%
FLV Sweet Coconut 1%
Posted to ELR by Pro_Vapes: http://e-liquid-recipes.com/recipe/239658

....

ULTIMATE CRUNCH BERRY CEREAL
FLV Cereal Crunch 3%
FW Tres Leches 3%
TPA Berry Crunch 2%
FLV Milk & Honey 1.5%
FLV Boysenberry 1%
FA Meringue 0.7%
FA Joy 0.3%
INW Lemon Mix 0.2% (Wera Garden brand)
FLV Coconut 0.1%
Posted to Reddit by Botboy141:
https://www.reddit.com/r/DIY_eJuice/comments/3ndybr/the_ulti-mate_crunch_berry_cereal_with_awesome/

....

CEREAL MILKS Posted By Tiffany Willey
FA Meringue 2%
FA Fresh Cream 0.5%
FA Caramel 2%
FW Yellow Cake 1%
FW Hazelnut 1%
TFA Banana Cream 1%
TFA Strawberry Ripe 3%
TFA Brown Sugar Extra 0.75%
TFA Graham Cracker (Clear) 1.25%
Add EM 10% Solution At 1% For More "Sugar" Flavour, Or Acetyl Pyrazine At 1% For More "Cereal" Flavour

....

TRIX AND MILK By Ashley Carter
TFA Silly Rabbit 4%
TFA Dairy Milk 4%
TFA Vanilla Swirl 3%
EM 10% Solution 1%
TFA Orange Cream 0.5%
Acetyl Pyrazine 0.15%
....

WHATAYOG By James Maybe
CAP Creamy Yoghurt 4%
FW Greek Yoghurt 3%
CAP French Vanilla v2 2%
CAP Sweet Cream 2%
INW Cherry 4%
TFA Meringue 1.5%
CAP Super Sweet 1%
FLV Sweet Coconut 1%
FLV Lemonade 0.5%
....

Yoghurt, Cereal, & Milk Style Recipes

Flavour	Steeping Time
Golden Grahams with Milk	3 Weeks
Strawberry Yoghurt Cheesecake	4 Weeks
Ultimate Crunch Berry Cereal	1 Week
Whatayog	7 Weeks

KREED'S KRISSMASS EGGNOG
CAP Eggnog 6%
CAP Marshmallow 5%
CAP Gingerbread 5%
TPA Jamaican Rum 3%
TPA Bavarian Cream 2%
TPA Cinnamon Spice 1%
....

SPICED HOT CHOCOLATE - CHRISTMAS MIX
TPA Dark Chocolate 1%
TPA Milk Chocolate 1%
TPA Bittersweet Chocolate 2%
TPA Chai Tea 1%
TPA Cinnamon 1%
LO Marshmallow 4%
TPA Malted Milk 5%
TPA Sweet Cream 5%
....

HOLIDAY EGGNOG (NEW)
FW or Cap Eggnog 6%
FA Jamaican Rum 1.5%
FA Marzipan 1%
TFA Brown Sugar (Extra) 2.5%
FA Cinnamon Ceylon .3%
FA Catalan Cream 1.5%
....

KAL'S SANTA HAT (NEW)
(Your Favourite) Bavarian Cream 2.25%
CAP Eggnog 6.50 %
CAP Gingerbread 5.5%
CAP Marshmallow 4.5%
Merry Christmas!
....

"OLD-FASHIONED" SPICED RUM CHRISTMAS FRUITCAKE

TPA RY4 Double 3%
FW Chocolate Hazelnut Spread 3%
FA Orange 0.5%
FW Butter Cream 0.25%
NF Pumpkin Spice 2%
INW Smoked Plum 0.125%
HS Dark Plum 0.125%
FA Bergamot 0.5%
TPA Cinnamon Spice 0.5%
FA Hazelnut 0.5%
FA Whipped Cream 0.125%
FA Black Pepper 0.25%
TPA Brown Sugar 0.5%
HS Lemon 0.5%
TPA Acetyl Pyrazine 0.5%
Sweetener 0.5%
Ethyl Maltol (10% Solution) 1%
Source: https://www.reddit.com/r/DIY_eJuice/comments/3lqh9d/oldfashioned_spiced_rum_christmas_fruitcake/

....

BOTBOY'S CHRISTMAS CUSTARD

TFA Pie Crust 3%
FA Coconut 1%
TFA Holiday Spice 1%
TFA Sweet Cream 3%
CAP Vanilla Custard V2 4%
TFA Peppermint 0.5%
FA Vienna Cream 1.5%
Source: https://www.reddit.com/r/DIY_eJuice/comments/2l0n6j/holiday_recipes_share_them_here/

....

WOLFPACK'S PUMPKIN PIE

CAP Pumpkin Pie 6%
FA Butterscotch 2%
CAP Whipped Cream 4%
TFA Bavarian Cream 5%
CAP Graham Cracker v2 3%
EM 10% Solution 1%
Source: https://www.reddit.com/r/DIY_eJuice/comments/2l0n6j/holiday_recipes_share_them_here/clsgq88

....

ALISA'S KRINGLE'S KURSE CLONE
TPA Creme de Menthe 3%
TPA Koolada 2%
CAP Menthol 2%
TPA Peppermint 8.5%
FW Sweetener 2%
Source: http://e-liquid-recipes.com/recipe/140696

....

QSPLAN'S FESTIVE LIQUID
Apple 10%
Eggnog 3%
Vanilla Custard 2%
Vanilla 1%
Cinnamon 2%
Maple Syrup 2%

Source: http://allaboute-cigarettes.proboards.com/thread/48856/xmas-festive-liquid

Apologies over there being no flavour brands on here, however, when I received the recipe there were none. I suggest using your preferred brands, and mixing up samplers.

....

Festive Recipes

Flavour	Steeping Time
Kreed's Krissmass Eggnog	2 Weeks
Kal's Santa Hat	3 Weeks

Kreed's Kollection of Recipes

Here you will find a kollection of vaping recipes by Kevin Reed (Kreed). Some of these may be in earlier chapters of the book, however, if you are looking for a recipe specifically from Kreed, this may be the easiest method for you.

KREED'S ANY FLAVOUR CAKEY YUMYUMS
FW Yellow Cake 4%
TPA Vanilla Cupcake 4%
TPA Bavarian Cream 4%
TPA Sweet Cream 4%
CAP Italian Lemon Sicily 4% OR
FA Lime Tahiti 4% It's Your Choice!
EM 10% Solution 2%

....

KREED'S BACCY
TPA DK Tobacco 3%
TPA Kentucky Bourbon 3%
TPA Hazelnut 3%
CAP Caramel 3%
CAP Marshmallow 2%
TPA Acetyl Pyrazine 1%
Saline 0.9% Solution 2 Drops Per 10Ml

....

KREED'S BACCY BLEND 2
TPA DK Tobacco 10%
TPA Coconut Extra 4%
TPA Vanilla Cupcake 4%
FW Caramel Salted 4%
CAP Double Chocolate 4%
CAP Peanut Butter 4%

....

KREED'S IRISH KISS
CAP Irish Cream 8%
TPA Peach 4%
CAP Caramel 4%
TPA Cinnamon Spice 1%
CAP Bavarian Cream 1%
TPA Smooth 1%
Breathe 12 Hours

....

KREED'S KRISSMASS EGGNOG
CAP Eggnog 6%
CAP Marshmallow 5%
CAP Gingerbread 5%
TPA Jamaican Rum 3%
TPA Bavarian Cream 2%
TPA Cinnamon Spice 1%

....

KREED'S KUSTARD
CAP Vanilla Custard v1 6%
CAP French Vanilla 4.5%
CAP New York Cheesecake 4.5%
CAP Ethyl Maltol 1%

To make 30ml of Kreed's Kustard to use as a one-shot, you will need the following:
CAP Vanilla Custard v1 11.25ml
CAP French Vanilla 8.45ml
CAP New York Cheesecake 8.45ml
CAP Ethyl Maltol 1.85ml
Use this in your PG, VG, and Nic at 16% for the mixing calculator, steeping time as above.

....

KREED'S MANGO DANISH PASTRY
TPA Mango 6%
CAP Maple Syrup 5%
TPA Brown Sugar 3.5%
TPA Toasted Almond 2%
TPA Cinnamon Danish 2%

....

KREED'S MELLOW MORNING
TPA Cappuccino 6%
TPA Sweet Cream 2%
CAP Marshmallow 2%
CV Brown Sugar 1%
(Kreed's Kommunication: You can play around with this a bit - leave out the sweet cream if you like black coffee. Leave out the brown sugar if you don't normally take it.
For an Irish coffee: Swap the sweet cream for CAP Irish Cream.)
....

KREED'S MR KIPLING'S BRAMLEY APPLE PIE
CAP Apple Pie 5%
TPA Green Apple 2%
TPA Sweet Cream 2%
TPA Pie Crust 1.5%
CAP Caramel 1.5%
CAP Vanilla Custard v1 1%
CAP French Vanilla 1%
TPA Dulce de Leche 1%
TPA Cinnamon Spice 1%
TPA Acetyl Pyrazine 1%
....

KREED'S PEACH AND RASPBERRY MELBA
TPA Peach 10%
VBL Raspberry 5%
TPA Vanilla Bean Gelato 5%
2 Week Steep
Optional: CAP Maple Syrup 1% Or Sweetener, Honey, Or Ethyl Maltol)
Koolada 10% Solution 2%
....

KREED'S PEANUT BUTTER CUP
CAP Peanut Butter 5%
CAP Double Chocolate 6%
TPA Malted Milk 3%
CAP Caramel 3%
CAP Graham Cracker 2%
Ethyl Maltol 1.5%
....

KREED'S PINEAPPLE UPSIDE DOWN CAKE
TPA Pineapple 10%
CAP Cake Batter 5%
CAP Maple Syrup 2%
TPA Brown Sugar Extra 2%
Ethyl Maltol 1%

....

KREED'S RASPBERRY RIPPLE
VBL Raspberry 10%
CAP Vanilla Custard 8%
TPA Vanillin 1%
TPA Koolada 3%
Ethyl Maltol 1%

....

KREED'S STRAWBERRY MILKSHAKE
TPA Strawberry Ripe 5%
CAP Sweet Strawberry 5%
CAP Vanilla Custard v1 5%
TPA French Vanilla 1.5%
TPA Bavarian Cream 1.5%
TPA Marshmallow 1.5%

....

KREED'S THICK BANANA MILKSHAKE
TPA DX Banana Cream 12%
CAP Vanilla Custard v1 5%
TPA Vanilla Custard 5%
TPA Malted Milk 3%
Ethyl Maltol 1%
(Kreed's Kommunication: The Two Custards Do Make A Difference, However, If You Don't Have One Or The Other, Use The One You Do Have At 10%)

....

KREED'S VAPERS TONGUE CURE
CAP Lemon Lime 13%
VBL Fennel 4%
VBL Pure Menthol 3%

....

Kreed's Kollection

Flavour	Steeping Time
Kreed's Any Flavour Cakey Yumyums	3 Weeks
Kreed's Baccy	4 Weeks
Kreed's Irish Kiss	4 Weeks
Kreed's Krissmass Eggnog	3 Weeks
Kreed's Kustard	6 Weeks
Kreed's Mango Danish Pastry	1 Week
Kreed's Mellow Morning	4 Weeks
Kreed's Mr Kipling's Bramley Apple Pie	3 Weeks
Kreed's Peanut Butter Cup	3 Weeks
Kreed's Pineapple Upside Down Cake	3 Weeks
Kreed's Raspberry Ripple	3 Weeks
Kreed's Strawberry Milkshake	4 Weeks
Kreed's Thick Banana Milkshake	3 Weeks

As members of Vaping Home Brewers will know, the group is unlike most other vaping groups, in that they do not have sponsors, do not allow vendors to advertise, and attempts to keep a distance from vendors in general. However, in partnership with Chef's Vapour, a small selection of recipes on VHB were turned into one shot concentrates, at no profit to either the group, nor Chef's. Now, the one shots will be generally available at standard retail pricing for all to enjoy.

In the spirit of the co-operative attitude of VHB, we asked vendors to either donate recipes, or discount codes. On the following pages you will find input from vendors who lurk in the VHB group. We have some recipes from well known juice vendors, and discount codes from home mixing suppliers. Any and all codes were correct at time of printing, and may be subject to minimum order values.

FROM DARK STAR:

DS-VHB 12% off everything at: www.darkstarvapour.co.uk
Many thanks to Rob Scammell.

CHEF'S VAPOUR RECIPES

STEAM GUNK'S FRUITION
CAP Blueberry 7%
CAP Cherry Wild 7%
TWG Blackcurrant 7%
INW Liquorice 1%

POSSET
CCW Lemon Grass 4%
CAP Coconut 8%
Capella Vanilla Custard v1 17%
TFA Bavarian Cream 2%
DV Lime Zinger 1%
EM 10% Solution 2%

....

STRAWBERRY RICE KRISPIES
FW Captain Crunch Berries 15%
CVR Strawberry milkshake 6%
CVR strawberry Vanilla 4%
CVR Vanilla Milkshake 2%
TPA Bavarian Cream 3%

....

SPICED PEAR
CAP Pear 12%
CAP Cinnamon Red Hot 8%
FA Cinnamon Spice 2%

....

DRUMSTICK
DV raspberry 7%
CC Cream 2%
Bavarian Cream 7%
EM 10% Solution 3%

....

A huge thanks to the guys at www.chefsvapour.co.uk for the recipes they have donated.

....

THE ECIG SHOP
  12% Discount on any purchase code - VHB12

STRAWBERRY AND WHITE CHOCOLATE CHEESECAKE By Craig Bradder
CAP Sweet Strawberry 8%
CAP NY Cheesecake 8%
TPA White chocolate 4%
FW Sweetener 3%
Steep for 7-10 days
....

STRAWBERRY AND RASPBERRY YOGHURT By Alan Hodgkinson
FW Yoghurt 6%
CAP Sweet Strawberry 4%
CAP Raspberry V2 4%
CAP Vanilla Custard V1 2%
TFA Bavarian Cream 2%
FW Sweetener 2%
....

  A huge thank you to the guys at http://thee-cigshop.co.uk/ for the code and recipes.
....

Appendix 1 - **Steeping**

WHAT IS STEEPING?
Steeping is the process of allowing the flavours to mix, and combine to give the best possible taste.

HOW DO YOU STEEP LIQUIDS?
The best possible steeping method to leave a juice in a room temperature, dark place. This reduces the amount the nicotine from oxidising, and changing the colour of the juice. Some juices will darken over time, even without nicotine.

There are many methods people will attempt to use to speed steep their juices, such as using a slow cooker, a saucepan of water, a microwave, USB cup warmers, and possibly others we have not yet encountered. There may be some truth to these, however, time is the best method out there.

If you do decide to try one of the heating methods, it is suggested that you leave the nicotine out of the juice until you have finished, as you will either break the nicotine down, or evaporate it, making it pointless having put it in, in the first place.

THERE ARE TWO MAJOR PROCESSES INVOLVED IN STEEPING E-LIQUID
1. Removal of volatile components by evaporation and degasification
This process would include the removal of alcohol but is not restricted to alcohol, there are other volatile components used in the production of flavour concentrates that generally give off an astringent or chemical odour. These process requires access to the atmosphere hence the need to remove tops from bottles.

1a Evaporation – This is the same process as used in cooking to remove alcohol from wine.

1b Degasification – This is the same process as letting a fizzy drink go flat

Both of these processes are accelerated by heat and increased surface area. This is a critical first step many e-Liquids are hideous and un-vapeable before this process. Without acceleration this can take a week or longer due to the viscosity of the liquid.

2. The Development Of Complex Flavour Molecules.
Over time some e-Liquids especially custard/caramel or desert flavours darken. From observation this cannot be oxidation as it occurs uniformly through the liquid and does not require agitation of the liquid to occur. It also cannot be caramelisation as this does not occur below 110°C.

MAILLARD REACTION - COLOUR AND FLAVOUR
What seems to be happening is a Maillard reaction commonly experienced by most people every day. The browning of bread, toast and potato chips, these are high temperature examples. Medium temperature examples creating Dulce de Leche and condensed milk.

Mallard reactions also occur at lower temperatures and contribute to the ageing of wine and Balsamic Vinegar.

Maillard reactions get exponentially slower as they progress. This fits in with our observations of steeping e-Liquid, a golden colour may be observed in a couple of days however the full desired flavour and colour may take 4-6 weeks to develop. The Maillard reactions will continue to progress over time, hence those almost black bottles of e-Liquid that are found at the back of a draw.

The degree of colour change is dependent on the type of flavours present and the presence of Nicotine. Some flavours wont change at all these are often referred to as shake and vape liquids. This mirrors the culinary world, you never see matured lemonade being sold.

ACCELERATING THE STEEPING PROCESS. REMOVAL OF VOLATILE COMPONENTS BY EVAPORATION AND DE-GASIFICATION

    A. Taking the top off the bottle.
    B. Shaking the bottle (Helps)
    C. Stirring (Helps)
    D. Whisking (Very effective)
    E. Blending to a foam (Super Effective)
    F. Ultrasonic degasification (Super Effective)

Appendix 2 - General Mixing Information

The mixing of e-cigarette juice should be undertaken on a non-porous surface, while wearing gloves suitable to protect your skin from contact with the liquids you are using.

Nicotine is a poison, it is toxic if swallowed or in contact with the skin. Please keep your concentrates locked up an away from children.
While mixing you may be using blunt needles with syringes. Please remember to treat these items with respect, they can still cause injury.

Please ensure that all your equipment has been sterilised in your preferred manner. For those that are new to mixing, you can sterilise your equipment in much the same way as you sterilise baby feeding equipment, such as steam, fluid, and boiling. Always select the most appropriate method for your equipment.

There may not be any practical difference between the pharmaceutical grade and food grade materials from some suppliers. The only difference might even be that the pharmaceutical grade is specially tested and comes with a test certificate.

However we do know that there is a difference between low-grade and high-grade materials in vaping products (though we cannot know what certificates / grades were supplied) because more tests are now showing MEG contamination - (mono)ethylene glycol - which is toxic, as is DEG. In fact it looks as if DEG contamination has been replaced by MEG contamination in the marketplace, perhaps because suppliers know to test for DEG but are unaware that low grade PG may contain MEG.

FLAVOUR PAIRINGS:

Some flavours will work when mixed, and others won't. While not an exhaustive guide, here are some examples of flavours that generally work well together, both in cooking, and vaping.

By all means, try flavours that are worlds apart. You never know, you might find something surprising and special.

Apple pairs well with: Caramel, Cardamom, Chestnut, Cinnamon, Cranberry, Currant, Ginger, Hazelnut, Mango, Maple, Rosemary, Walnut.

Apricot pairs well with: Almond, Black Pepper, Caramel, Cardamom, Ginger, Hazelnut, Honey, Orange, Peach, Vanilla, Plum.

Asian Pear pairs well with: Almond, Apple, Black Pepper, Cinnamon, Ginger, Honey, Macadamia, Nutmeg, Raisin, Vanilla.

Banana pairs well with: Caramel, Cherry, Chocolate, Cinnamon, Coffee, Ginger, Hazelnut, Honey, Mango, Molasses, Papaya.

Blackberry pairs well with: Apricot, Black Pepper, Cinnamon, Citrus, Hazelnut, Lemon, Other Berries, Peach, Plum.

Blood Orange pairs well with: Almond, Cardamom, Chocolate, Cinnamon, Clove, Fig, Ginger, Honey, Other Citrus.

Blueberry pairs well with: Other Berries, Cardamom, Mango, Lemon, Hazelnut, Ginger, Fig, Lavender, Other Citrus.

STORING YOUR JUICE:

The proper storage of e Liquid can have a huge impact on the taste and integrity of the eLiquid sitting in your house. Since taste plays a huge factor with any vaping experience, it is essential to take the time to understand how eLiquid can be stored to retain its maximum flavour.

The first major factor in storing e Liquid is the container itself. Most eLiquids are sold in plastic containers, which manufacturers prefer because plastic is resilient and cheap. While this is fine for short term storage, plastic tends to leave a distinctive aftertaste in the eLiquid if stored inside these containers for too long. A better option is glass, which does not interact with the eLiquid in the same fashion. Make sure the glass bottle or vial has a lid that can be screwed on to keep air out. This will also preserve the freshness of the liquid, we also recommend a childproof lid if you have, or are in regular contact with children.

The storage container is only one factor. It is also important to pick a location that is cool. Some people take this advice to the extreme and store their eLiquid in the refrigerator or freezer. But in reality, these extreme temperatures are bad for the product. In fact, extreme temperatures can actually affect the chemical makeup of the eLiquid and render it useless. For the best results in storing your eLiquid, room temperature is often the best choice. Additionally, many people have success storing their eLiquid in basements where the air is cool but not cold. Cabinets, cupboards and closets are also good options.

If eLiquid is stored in a refrigerated space (which we don't recommend), be sure to let it air out prior to use in order to minimise the effects of the cooling process. As a general rule, eLiquid should always be used at room temperature in order to experience the best results.

When it is frozen or chilled, the liquid tends to get oily and thick, which can impede the quality of the product in use.

Similarly, direct heat is also bad for eLiquid. You should take measures to ensure that your eLiquid is never exposed to direct sunlight for any period of time. This means it is important to avoid windows and other places where light and sun are of particular concern. Many people use dark tinted glass bottles in order to provide further light protection for their eLiquid.

Appendix 3 - Kreed's Mixing Tips

KREED'S NO1 TIP FOR BUDDING RECIPE CREATORS
TRY YOUR FLAVOURS

I'm willing to bet that most of you have a lot of concentrates that you have never tried as standalone flavours. It's no good just seeing a recipe, buying the concentrates and making it up.

You may end up with a decent e-liquid, but you learned nothing. A lick test will also only tell you so much, you need to make a 5ml sample at 0mg (to keep cost down) and vape it.

Most manufacturers state recommended percentages so use those as a start point. If you want to develop your own mixing skills, you have to start with the basics.

KREED'S NO2 TIP FOR BUDDING RECIPE CREATORS
NOTHING IS EVER WASTED

If you follow on from my tip earlier about creating small samples with 0mg then, GOOD NEWS! Even if you don't like it as a vape you need to remember this simple thing:
FAILED MIXES CAN BE USED ELSEWHERE!

These are food flavourings. Add 4 or 5 drops to a coffee or a hot chocolate, try a few drops in Coke or Pepsi, or a martini! Try some in ice cream, puddings or whipped cream. These things are awesome for diabetics, no sugar, carbs, fat or calories.

FINAL TIP FOR USING THESE.

Make a bottle of NEVER AGAIN juice. Throw every failed mix you have into one bottle and shake the hell out of it, then try it.

The best juice I vape at home is one of these, but when it's gone it's gone, boo-hoo.

KREED'S NO3 TIP FOR BUDDING RECIPE CREATORS
NICOTINE DOES NOT NEED TO STEEP!

Make your new/untried recipes up, leave out the nicotine, label with how much of your nicotine base you still need to add, and steep in your usual method.

That way you only need to add the most expensive ingredient at the end, and only IF you like the recipe. It has nothing to do with nicotine degradation or anything like that.

It's just about saving you money.

KREED'S NO4 TIP FOR BUDDING RECIPE CREATORS
START SMALL

I cannot remember how many times I've seen this post:

"I mixed 250ml of this and it's crap"

What a waste eh?

This is similar to the KNOW YOUR FLAVOURS tip in that you should be trying recipes in MAX 10ml amounts first.

TASTE IS SUBJECTIVE

Just because someone else has said: "This recipe is awesome!" There is still no guarantee that you're going to like it.

A 10ml mix is a far better idea than a desperate post that says: "My mix tastes crap, what else can I add to it to make it better?"

Again, this is about saving you money. So before you dive in with another 250ml mix… START SMALL.

Appendix 4 - Nicotine

NICOTINE ABSORPTION

One of the most common misconceptions in the vaping world (for both new and advanced vapers) is nicotine absorption. Commonly, new vapers will be directed towards higher concentrated e-juices (18mg+) and more experienced vapers tend to gravitate towards 12mg and less.

Generally, this is thought to be due to addiction levels and nicotine tolerance. However, this is where the misconception begins, and this information is what (hopefully) will end it!

When a new vaper suddenly switches to electronic cigarettes they generally start with a lower end device such as an eGo and CE4 combo. As they graduate further into vaping, they'll end up with better atomisers/cartomisers/RBAs and more powerful mods. This plays a small role in the nicotine dispersion as a mod with a powerful atomiser will, of course, produce more vapour and thus deliver more nicotine. However, if you were to give a new vaper a quad-coil RBA and mechanical mod; chances are they'd still require more nicotine than the advanced vaper. Why? Technique. People who recently came off of cigarettes tend to take quick, short drags on the electronic cigarette which results in little nicotine absorption; so they require much more nicotine in their e-juice to reach a satisfied state. An advanced vaper knows to take long, slow pulls which results in a higher amount of nicotine absorbed (*and likewise, a lesser need for high strength nicotine e-juices). It doesn't end here!

A study was conducted where advanced vapers were given one hour to vape on starter ecigs and advanced ecigs. After the hour they had blood tests done which showed that they still hadn't received enough nicotine (using 18mg e-juice) as they would have within FIVE MINUTES of smoking a traditional cigarette! That's amazing! In fact, you'd need a 50mg e-juice to match what you would have gotten out of five minutes of smoking!

Nicotine absorption through vaping is exceedingly lower than what is received out of smoking a traditional cigarette and most of the e-juices you'll find on the market don't even come relatively close to being enough to equal the nicotine you received in your cigarettes.

(Please note: we are not recommending that you vape 50mg e-juice!)

Another study suggests that the amount of nicotine absorbed is 1/10 of what is promised due to nicotine burning off through the vaporising process. A follow-up study was conducted with vapers over the course of 5 hours in which they were able to vape for one hour at their leisure, and their nicotine absorption was fair - keeping in mind that we were not given the variables of their vaping (excessive, moderate, light, etc) to reach a decent absorption rate. Therefore, this is largely why we find that we vape much more than we ever smoked, and sometimes can drag a vape session out into an hour (or more) just to feel satisfied! The nicotine absorption just isn't there - especially for new vapers whose bodies are still accustomed to taking in massive amounts of nicotine and absorbing it successfully. There is a benefit to this: as we vape, our nicotine dependency will naturally lower, which is another reason why experienced vapers do not require such high levels of nicotine in their juices.

Nicotine WILL NOT degrade if it is 100% pure and nitrogen sealed in dark glass bottles and kept at a low temperature. That's how professional labs keep it so it's as close as a fact as you will get when it comes to nicotine storage! Obviously you aren't going to be able to achieve all those criteria at home (you wont have 100% pure nicotine being the main one) BUT majority of us could accomplish two of those important criteria.

Once you add other chemicals such as PG or VG into the bottle and can't remove all the oxygen then degradation occurs. At what rate and the effect is open to question as no one has actually kept PG or VG nicotine base in a freezer for more than about 5 years so far but it will degrade to some degree even if you do keep it in your freezer. The issue really is with the oxygen either from air trapped in the bottle or through energy put into the chemical system via light (UV) breaking down the dilutant (PG or VG), which unfortunately being organic compounds have oxygen in their make up. It's fine normally because the oxygen in the dilutant is attached to a hydrogen, making a diol (O-H) and will not compete for the nicotine but if you add energy into the system the one single covalent bond between the oxygen and the hydrogen can be broken and you have the issue of the spare oxygen running around causing problems. This is the reason to keep the nicotine base in amber glass bottles and is the same reason that nicotine is kept nitrogen sealed in labs - so there are no spare oxygen atoms. Keeping the nicotine base at low (freezer) temperatures also slows down the movement of the molecules, which obviously slows down any chemical reactions.

Oxygen is nicotine's main enemy, it converts it to nicotine oxide in an oxidation reaction and nicotine oxide being a charged molecule has free electrons, this is why the colour change occurs (free electron movement between the atomic energy levels). These free electrons can also target other substances in e-liquid such as flavourings and changes their chemical structure, which coincidentally is the reason why e-liquid has a shelf life.

STORAGE BASICS
Always buy the highest percentage nicotine base you can buy (currently 7.2% (72mg) legally in the UK) as the less PG/VG you have in the bottle the better and always buy the best quality, freshest base you can find to start off with.

WHAT TO STORE IT IN?
Nicotine base should be stored in dark amber glass bottles to stop UV degradation and potential chemical leaching caused by plastic bottles.

HOW TO STORE IT?
Depending on your usage if you bought 1 litre+ bottles then you should decant it into smaller quantity bottles containing the amount you would probably use in 3 or 4 months so that you aren't exposing the majority of the nicotine base to more oxygen every time you want to use it. Once you open a bottle it's best to store it in a fridge if possible rather than just a shelf at room temperature and ALWAYS out of sunlight. It is worth noting that PG nicotine base remains fairly free flowing even straight out of the freezer but VG base turns into a gel and will need several hours at room temperature to be useable.

WHERE IN THE FREEZER TO STORE IT?
Purely from a safety point of view it is best to store it at the bottom of the freezer so that if it does leak it doesn't contaminate anything else in the freezer. I know that some people have a separate freezer for their nicotine base but plenty just stick it in with rest of the families shopping! Make sure that the bottle is clearly labelled, not for you but for the other people using the freezer. If you have young children it would be very wise, if not essential, to buy a small freezer to keep in the garage or similar just for your nicotine stocks.

WHAT'S BETTER, PG OR VG AS THE DILUENT?
A personal preference really but concerning degradation then VG has an extra O-H functional group (3 compared to 2 in PG) so it is possible that if degradation did take place it would be quicker in the VG. However VG has a better shelf life than PG, 2 years compared to 1 year generally AND VG's viscosity works in it's favour for once as the more viscous a liquid the less the molecules move about ...... So it's probably 6 of one half a dozen of the other really as to which is best!

HOW LONG WILL IT LAST?

It would be expected to possibly see and experience noticeable degradation after 5 -10 years storage either in taste or colour. Strength drop would need chemical analysis once someone has stored it for that long to determine but it is believed by many that it won't be anywhere near half.

WHAT NOT TO DO

Leave the bottles alone! The less they are disturbed the better. DO NOT open the bottles if you don't need to and never shake them as this introduces oxygen to more of the nicotine base rather than just the surface.

I am not a qualified Industrial Chemist. This information has been obtained from conversations with qualified Industrial Chemists and personal experience and is for information only. I recommend you use this information as the basis for your own research rather than the definitive guide to Nicotine Base storage.

THE COLOUR OF YOUR NICOTINE EXPLAINED (BY KAL MORRIS):

I am frequently asked about the colouring of my nicotine, if the colour is an indication of the strength or quality of the nicotine or if the colour has any impact (positive or negative) on the nicotine at all. The short answer is no.

In "Analytical Determination of Nicotine and Related Compounds and their Metabolites" by J.W. Gorrod and P. Jacob III they state, "[...]Pure nicotine is a colourless liquid with a characteristic acrimonious odour.

Nicotine boils at 246-247C. On exposure to air and light, or even on standing in the dark in a sealed bottle, over time the colourless or pale yellow oily liquid becomes the brownish colour of stored nicotine. Brown coloured nicotine is as toxic as pure colourless or pale yellow nicotine[...]" indicating that the colour change in nicotine is a direct result of age. (Source:http://www.v-ecigs.com/nicotine -- you can read a lot of the book while you're there, too!) As the nicotine ages it'll come into contact with light, heat and oxygen which will also contribute to a colour change.

There are two primary methods of nicotine extraction: the first, and most common in pharmaceutical grade manufacturers, is the distillation process. In this process they remove the natural impurities from the plant based liquid and leave you with the nicotine liquid. The alternative practice is to utilise salt processing and turn the liquid into a sulphate. This requires a bleaching agent to remove the impurities and then is reconstituted with a liquid to turn it back into a useable form. Bleached liquid appears to be more clear and is therefore is frequently mistaken as being more pure. In fact, the nicotine that goes through the distillation process is more refined. Regardless of method, the colour of the nicotine is purely cosmetic and plays no real determining factor in judging which is purer or of higher quality.

A common concern with nicotine is that the coloration determines the strength of the nicotine. Frequently I will receive questions asking if I sent the wrong concentration due to the colouring being either lighter or darker than the last shipment. The colour change can be because of age and environmental factors that do not affect the nicotine's potency, but we've found another reason for the colour change: because nicotine has high acidity, it will alter the chemical structure of the flavouring and cause a colour change. As time goes and the liquid becomes oxidised, the colour will become darker.

Appendix 5 - Common Abbreviations

FOR CONCENTRATE MANUFACTURERS

CAP = Capella

INA/INW =Inawera

TPA/TFA = The Perfumers Apprentice/The Flavourers Apprentice

FA = Flavourart

FW = Flavourwest

DV = Decadant Vapours

M+P = Moms and Pops

OOO = One-on-One Flavours

PSV/PS = Pink Spot Vapours

TP = Tasty Puff

CK = Classikool

TWG = Totally Wicked Gold

KH = Kandi-hed

LO/LA = Lor Ann

FLV = Flavourah

CCW = Cup Cake World

CV/CC/CHC = Chef's Vapour Own/Chefs Choice

VV = Vampire Vapes

CVR - Chef's Rebranded

JF - Juice Factory

TJ - T-Juice

CJ - Ciggy Juice

FJ - Flavour Junkie

NF - Nature's Flavours

TDM - Tino D'Milano

VBL - Vapeable

HS - Hangsen

CI - Cuts Ice

LL - Leisure Liquids

BJ - Big Juice

FE - Flavour Express

VD - Vape Domain

Appendix 6 - Guides to Average Percentages

FOR BRANDED CONCENTRATES

The following percentages are a guideline only sourced from user info and maker recommendations personal taste and mixing ratios play a great part.

CAPELLA

Amaretto 6%To 8%
Apple Pie 7% To 9%
Banana 17% To 21%
Blueberry 16% To 20%
Banana Split 7% To 9%
Blueberry 16% To 20%
Blueberry Cinnamon Crumble 8% To 12%
Blue Raspberry Cotton Candy 8% To 12%
Boston Cream Pie 15% To 20%
Bull Horn 9% To 12%
Cappuccino 10%To 12%
Cherry Cola 14% To 16%
Choc Glazed Doughnut 8% To 11%
Chocolate Fudge Brownie 8% To 11%
Chocolate Raspberry 18% To 20%
Cranberry 10% To 12%
Double Chocolate Mint 9% To 11%
Egg Nog 8% To 10%
Hot Cocoa 7% To 10%
Irish Cream 6% To 8%
Popcorn 10 To 12%
Pineapple And Cream 8% To 11%
Sweet Guava 8% To 10%
Sweet Tangerine 13% To 16%
Vanilla Cupcake 7% To 10%
Vanilla Custard 12% To 14%

DECADENT VAPOURS

....

Absinthe 7% To 8%
American Red 9% To 12%
Apple 14% To 16%
Banana 9% To 11%
Black Cherry 9% To 11%
Blackcurrant 9% To 11%
Caramel 10% To 14%
Cherry Ice 11% To 13%
Choc Caramel 12% To 15%
Coconut Ice 10% To 12%
Cola Kick 10% To 12%
Dy3 15%
Dy4 15%
Gingerbread 11% To 14%
Line Zinger 11% To 14%
Parma Violet 10% To 12%
Raspberry 12% To 14%

FLAVOURART

....

Almond 2% To 5%
Anise 4% T0 6%
Apple 4% To 6%
Apricot 3% To 6%
Banana 4% To 7%
Beer 5%
Bilberry 2% To 4%
Black Cherry 4% To 6%
Black Tea 4% To 6%
Blackberry 3% To 5%
Blackcurrant 3% To 5%
Brandy 2% To 4%
Butterscotch 3% To 5%
Cappuccino 4% To 5%
Caramel 4% To 6%
Catalan Cream 4% To 6%
Cherry 6% To 8%
Chocolate 5% To 7%
Cinnamon 4% To 5%
Citrus Mix 4% To 8%
Cocoa 4% To 6%
Coconut 6% To 9%

Coffee Expresso 2.5% To 4.5%
Cola 4% To 7%
Cookie 3.5% To 5.5%
Cream Fresh 4%
Cream Whipped 4%
Custard 5% To 7%
Fig 4% To 5%
Forest Fruit 4% To 7%
Green Tea 3% To 4%
Guava 3% To 5%
Hazelnut 3% To 5%
Honey 4% To 6%
Irish Cream 3% To 4%
Kiwi 4% To 5%
Liquorice 4% To 5%
Cold Pressed Lime 4%
Lime Tahity 3% To 4%
Lychee 4% To 6%
Mad Fruit 5%
Mandarin 6%
Mango 5% To 8%
Marshmallow 4% To 5%
Menthol Arctic 2% To 4%
Nut Mix 3%
Orange 5% To 6%
Passion Fruit 4% To 5%
Peach 4% To 5%
Peanut 3% To 5%
Pear 4% To 7%
Peppermint 3% To 5%
Pineapple 5% To 9%
Pomegranate 3% To 4%
Raspberry 6% To 9%
Red Bull 3% To 5%
Spearmint 5% To 6%
Strawberry 2% To 3.5%
Tiramasu 4% To 6%
Tutti Frutti 2% To 4%
Vanilla Bourbon 5% To 8%
Walnut 4% To 6%
Whiskey 3% To 4%

FLAVOURWEST

....

American Coke 12% To 15%
Apricot 14% To 17%
Banana 12% To 15%
Banana Foster 12% To 15%
Banana Nut Bread 9% To 11 %
Black Liquorice 11% To 13%
Black Cherry 16% To 18%
Bubble Gum 14% To 16%
Butter Rum 10% To 13%
Butter Popcorn 10% To 13%
Cake Yellow 14% To 16%
Cappuccino 11% To 14%
Caramel Candy 14% To 16%
Cinnamon Red Hot 6% To 8%
Cinnamon Roll 14% To 16%
Coconut Cream Pie 12% To 15%
Coffee 9% To 11%
Cookies And Cream 16% To 20%
Cotton Candy 14% To 16 %
Cream Soda 13% To 15%
Double Apple 15% To 17%
Doublemint Gum 14% To 16%
Ecto Cooler 15% To 18%
Guava 11% To 14%
Gummy Bear 9% To 11%
Hazelnut 12% To 15%
Jungle Juice 12% To 14%
Key Lime 15% To 20%
Lemonade 9% To 11%
0Range 15% To 17%
Orange Dream Bar 14% To 16%
Peach 13% To 16%
Peanut Butter 15% To 18%
Pineapple 14% To 16%
Pink Champagne 13% To 15%
Plumb 13% To 15%
Ruby Red Grapefruit 13% To 15%
Snickers Type 14% To 16%
Swiss Cherry 12% To 15%
Tangerine 15% To 18%
Tropical Punch 14% To 16%
Vanilla Custard 14% To 16%
Waffle 18% To 20%
White Chocolate 15% To 18%

INAWERA FLAVOURS

Banana 4% To 6%
Blackberry 4% To 6%
Cappuccino 4% To 6%
Cola 3% To 5%
Cool Mint 3% To 4%
Hazelnut 3% To 5%
Honey 3% To 4%
Grape 3% To 4%
Lemon 3% To 4%
Milk Chocolate 5% To 8%
Mint 3% To 5%
Nougat 6% To 8%
Orange 3.5% To 4.5%
Peanut 3% To 5%
Plum 4% To 5%
Raspberry 3% To 5%
Two Apples 4% To 6%
Lemon 4% To 6%

....

Absinthe 5% To 8%
Apple 12% To 14%
Banana Cream 15% To 20%
Blackberry 14% To 16%
Black Cherry 9% To 12%
Caramel Original 16% To 20%
Caramel Candy 15% To 18%
Chai Tea 8% To 10%
Cinnamon Danish 8% To 10%
Coffee 4% To 7%
Creme De Mint 5% To 7%
Dragon Fruit 9% To 11%
Double Chocolate 4% To 6%
French Vanilla 7% To 10%
Gingerbread 8% To 11%
Granny Smith 7% To 9%
Green Tea 5% To 7%
Hazelnut 9% To 11%
Honey 6.5% To 8.5%
Lemon 9% To 11%
Mary Jane 14% To 16%
Milk Chocolate 8% To 11%
Mocha 5% To 7%
Passion Fruit 9% To 12%
Pineapple 11% To 13%
Pina Colada 5% To 6%
Popcorn 14% To 16%
Raspberry 11% To 14%
Ripe Banana 14% To 16%
Ry4 13% To 15%
Strawberry And Cream 9% To 12%
Waffel 10% To 14%

TASTY PUFF

Awesome Apple 2% To 4%
Blueberry Thrill 3.5% To 5%
California Orange 2% To 3%
Chick Magnet Cherry 4% To 4%
Chumpy Chocolate 4% To 5%
Chronic Hypnotic 4% To 5%
Convicted Melon (Melone) 4% To 6%
Crazy Coconut 2% To 4%
Electric Banana 4% To 6%
Flower Power 3% To 4%
Jungle Juice 4% To 6%
Mango Tango 4% To 5%
Mr Bubble 4% To 6%
Pimpy Fresh Peach 4% To 6%
Purple Haze 3% To 4%
Rasta Rootbeer 3% To 4%
Rippin' Raspberry 4% To 6%
Silly Strawberry 3% To 5%
Sinful Cinnamon 4% To 5%
Spiffy Spearmint 3% To 4%
Toke A Cola 5% To 6%

TOTALLY WICKED GOLD

Blue Hawaii 5% To 7%
Ice Menthol 3% To 4%
Iron Brewed 3% To 4%

Appendix 7 - Additives

Many additives for e-liquid can be purchased in powder, crystal or granule form that can then be suspended in PG to form a solution.
Add 1 gram of the powder to 9ml of PG to form a 10% solution and 2 grams to 9ml of PG to form a 20% solution (this isn't exact but its close enough for our purposes)

ETHYL MALTOL

TPA/TFA sells this as Cotton Candy. Usually comes in crystal form. To make a 10% solution, use one part EM-crystals and 9 parts PG, mix, shake until dissolved completely. Usually gentle heating speeds up the process. An easy way is to microwave for 3 seconds, shake until cooled down, and repeat until completely dissolved.

ETHYL VANILLIN

as ethyl maltol

KOOLADA

Menthyl methyl lactate, also known as Koolada is usually in a 10% solution. If you like the cooling effect that menthol has, but don't want the actual flavour, Koolada adds that cooling effect of menthol but without the flavour. Use sparingly around 0.5-4%

CITRIC ACID (SOME USE JIF LEMON)

Again, a 10% solution. Increases acidity. Used to enhance fruity flavours and give it "that something extra". Typical dosage: 1-2 drops per 5 ml liquid.

Initially, mixes with lemon juice appear to have better flavour, but over time tend to have more muted flavours.

MALIC ACID

Typically in a 20% solution, 2g crystals to 8ml PG. It adds a sour note. At 1-2 drops per 10 ml liquid, it tends to enhance (to "pop") fruity flavours. At larger percentages it makes a "sour candy" effect. TFA/TPA sells this as Sour.

TRIMETHYL PYRAZINE

Usually in a 10% solution, trimethyl pyrazine is good for tobacco mixes. Taste notes attributed: Nutty, musty, cocoa, drying, peanut-like and raw coffee. Use sparingly! Add 1 drop per 10 ml and add to taste.

The Perfumer's Apprentice has it, others may too.

MENTHOL

You can buy menthol crystals lots of places. It's easy to make your own menthol liquid from the crystals. The easiest way is to grind the crystals up real fine, then fill a bottle half full (or just under), and then add your PG or VG. Shake vigorously. Warm water bath may help dissolve it. If you use VG you will not be able to dissolve as much as with PG, and you stand a chance that crystallisation may occur.

Appendix 8 - Volume 1 Steeping Tables

Drinks or Alcohol Inspired Recipes

Flavour	Steeping Time
Cherry Ameretto	1 Week
Tasty Strawberry Milkshake	2 Weeks
Strawberry Soda	3 Days
Strawberry Limeade	2 Days
Hard Lemonade	10 Days
Xtreme Cola	10 Days
Vimtoish	1 Week
Karakof Cream	2 Weeks

Fruit or Fruity Style Recipes

Flavour	Steeping Time
Pearnana	3 Days
Triple Melon Mix	1 Week
Crystal Lite	10 Days
Melon Chilli	2 Days
Strawpeary	1 Day
Creamy Mango and Pineapple	2 Weeks
Gone Bananas	2 Days
Wild Bunch	1 Week
Red, Blue, and Peachy	1 Week
Berry Medley Yoghurt	6 Weeks
Pineapple Cream	10 Days
Bangin' Orange	2 Weeks
Vacation Mix	2 Days
Juicy Fruit Chewing Gum	3 Days

Fruit or Fruity Style Recipes Cont

Flavour	Steeping Time
Voodoo	2 Days

Yoghurt, Cereal and Milk Style Recipes

Flavour	Steeping Time
Crunchberries	1 Week

Dessert Style Recipes

Flavour	Steeping Time
Cattlebrosia	2 Weeks
Sweet Honey Waffles	2 Weeks
Creamy Caramel	10 Days
Pineapple Cheesecake	3 Weeks
Black Forest Cake	2 Weeks

Tobacco Recipes-1

Flavour	Steeping Time
Smoking Snake	5 Days
Gingerbread Backy	10 Days

Miscellaneous Recipes-1

Flavour	Steeping Time
A Pair of Dragons	4 Weeks
Skittles	10 Days
Swedish Fish	10 Days
Ice Ice Baby	2 Days
Peanut Butter Surprise	10 Days
Cool Monster	1 Week

Clone Recipes-1

Flavour	Steeping Time
Mother's Milk Clone	4 Weeks
Milkman Clone	3 Days
Muffin Man Clone	1 Week
Andromeda Style	2 Weeks

Notes

Notes

Notes

Glossary

E-Juice, E-Liquid, Home Brew - The liquid used for vaping, and whether it was purchased from a vendor, or mixed at home by yourself.

VG - Vegetable Glycerin, a base liquid that provides a smoother vaping experience, and increases the volume, and thickness of "clouds". Very thick and viscous, needs thinning with other liquids for most tank systems.

PG, MPG - Mono-Propylene Glycol - An excellent flavour carrier, provides the "throat hit" some vapers are looking for to associate with smoking. Normally used to thin down VG for tanks.

AG - Aqueous Glycerin. VG mixed with Distilled Water, to thin the VG down for those who may be intolerant to PG. You cannot use tap water, deionised water, or bottled water. You need to ensure it is distilled for safety.

Nic, Nicotine - an ingredient in e-juice that satisfies the craving when coming from smoking cigarettes. Nicotine is a poison in high concentrations, either ingested or through skin contact, so gloves are recommended. The highest mg/ml available in the UK is 72mg/ml, while in the USA and other countries 100mg/ml is available. In percentages, you are looking at 7.2% and 10%. You cannot buy 100% nicotine without the correct licenses. Nicotine is available suspended in either VG or PG.

Concentrates - Flavours used to give e-juice it's distinctive taste. Not vapable on their own. All vaping flavours are food flavourings, either designed to avoid ingredients that could cause health issues, such as certain oils, or straight as they are. Most are natural flavours, suspended in PG. VG flavourings are available, however vapers have reported them to be muted compared to PG based flavourings.

Steeping - In the context of vaping, steeping has become known as the process of allowing the flavours of the concentrates to blend with the base liquids.

Additives - There are many additives available as either liquid solutions or in powder or crystal forms. The effects of these on health is unknown, and therefore should be used sparingly, and only when needed.

Mixing Percentages - All recipes are expressed in mixing percentages, which you can input on one of many mixing calculators available for free on the internet. It tells you the ratio of each flavour that needs to be used for best results.

One Shots - A One Shot is a pre blended concentrate of a certain flavour, meaning you can purchase a single flavour, as opposed to many flavours you may not use again, thus allowing you to trial a flavour, before investing in many different ones.

Recipe Index

www.ingramcontent.com/pod-product-compliance
Lightning Source LLC
Chambersburg PA
CBHW071355280526
45787CB00001B/341